I0760227

William Morgan

UNIVERSITY PRESS OF FLORIDA

Florida A&M University, Tallahassee

Florida Atlantic University, Boca Raton

Florida Gulf Coast University, Ft. Myers

Florida International University, Miami

Florida State University, Tallahassee

New College of Florida, Sarasota

University of Central Florida, Orlando

University of Florida, Gainesville

University of North Florida, Jacksonville

University of South Florida, Tampa

University of West Florida, Pensacola

WILLIAM MORGAN

Evolution of an Architect

RICHARD SHIELDHOUSE

Foreword by Martha Kohen

University Press of Florida
Gainesville · Tallahassee · Tampa · Boca Raton
Pensacola · Orlando · Miami · Jacksonville · Ft. Myers · Sarasota

Printed in Korea on acid-free paper

This book may be available in an electronic edition.

23 22 21 20 19 18 6 5 4 3 2 1

Library of Congress Control Number: 2017952797
ISBN 978-0-8130-5690-6

The University Press of Florida is the scholarly publishing agency for the State University System of Florida, comprising Florida A&M University, Florida Atlantic University, Florida Gulf Coast University, Florida International University, Florida State University, New College of Florida, University of Central Florida, University of Florida, University of North Florida, University of South Florida, and University of West Florida.

University Press of Florida
15 Northwest 15th Street
Gainesville, FL 32611-2079
http://upress.ufl.edu

Contents

List of Figures vii

Foreword xi

Introduction 1

1 Early Years 7

2 Harvard College 13

3 Navy Service 19

4 Harvard Graduate School of Design 26

5 A Career Begins 51

6 The Practice Expands 89

7 Trailblazing in Earth Architecture 117

8 Bold Design on a Large Scale 133

9 Author and Architect 161

10 More Recent Projects 183

11 Final Thoughts 198

Afterword 205

Acknowledgments 217

Notes 221

Bibliography 223

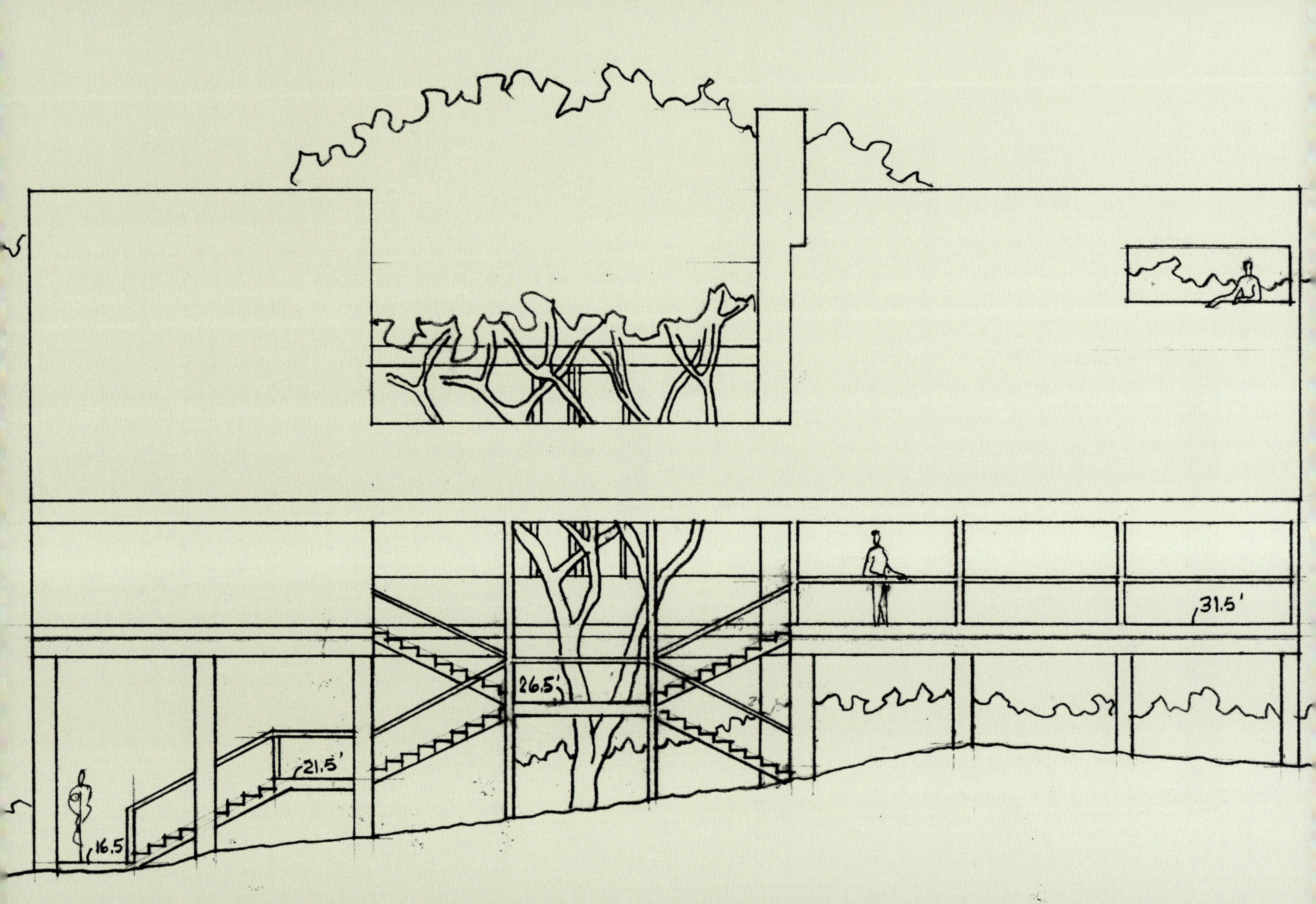
31.5'
26.5'
21.5'
16.5

Figures

1. William Morgan and brother, Thomas, on tricycles 10
2. Morgan with Fletcher High School teammates 11
3. High school portrait of Morgan 11
4. William Morgan demonstrating his sling chair 16
5. Patent for "sling-type chair" 17
6. Morgan during ROTC cruise 18
7. Morgan on duty in the Pacific 20
8. Bunny and William Morgan's engagement party 22
9. The wedding of Bunny and William Morgan 22
10. Architecture student at Harvard 27
11. Guam Vacation House, sketch 37
12. Guam Vacation House, drawing 38
13. Morgan presenting to a GSD jury 39
14. Morgan with Michael Zimmer and Nelson Chin 39
15. Drawing of a community center 43
16. Project concerning an elementary school 44
17. National Cowboy Hall of Fame, drawing for design competition 46
18. National Cowboy Hall of Fame, drawing 47
19. Toronto City Hall, design competition entry 49
20. Toronto City Hall, model and GSD students 49
21. The Morgan family 50
22. William and Bunny Morgan in Venice 50
23. 1611 Ocean Boulevard, Atlantic Beach 53
24. 1611 Ocean Boulevard, interior 53
25. 1611 Ocean Boulevard, contemporary view 54
26. Former Maryland Fried Chicken building 57
27. E.L.K. Oil Company Building, foreshadowing sketches 59

28. E.L.K. Oil Company Building, construction 59
29. E.L.K. Oil Company Building, preparing roof sections 60
30. E.L.K. Oil Company Building, contemporary view 61
31. Novelty postcard from Peru 62
32. Page from an unpublished draft of a book 64
33. Rawls Residence, east side 66
34. Rawls Residence, circular stairway off second floor 67
35. Rawls Residence, early sketch 67
36. Rawls Residence, contemporary view 68
37. Rawls Residence, contemporary interior view 69
38. Williamson Residence, Ponte Vedra Beach 70
39. Williamson Residence, drawing 70
40. Williamson Residence, hurricane damage 71
41. Goodloe Residence, Ponte Vedra Beach 73
42. Goodloe Residence, early sketch 74
43. Goodloe Residence, terrace 74
44. Goodloe Residence, modules in "pinwheel" formation 75
45. "Multi-story trailer park," early drawing 78
46. Interpod application, model 78
47. Interpod design 79
48. Seaplace, courtyard 82
49. Seaplace, aerial view soon after construction 83
50. Morgan and drawing of the original Place by the Sea project 83
51. Seaplace, wall separating it from the beach 86
52. Seaplace, blocked view corridors 87
53. Jacksonville Children's Museum, main entrance 92
54. Jacksonville Children's Museum, elevation 93
55. Jacksonville Children's Museum, early sketches 93
56. Jacksonville Children's Museum, contemporary view 95
57. Florida State Museum, view looking west 97
58. Florida State Museum, view along Museum Drive 98
59. Florida State Museum, Morgan with model 98
60. Florida State Museum, contemporary view 100
61. Florida State Museum, terraces 102
62. Florida State Museum, stairs up earthen berm 103
63. William Morgan Residence, view from the south 105
64. William Morgan Residence, site plan 106
65. William Morgan Residence, interior 106
66. William Morgan Residence, garden 107
67. William Morgan Residence, contemporary view 108
68. William Morgan Residence, contemporary view of garden 108

69. Dickinson Residence, view from the west 110
70. Dickinson Residence, view from beach 111
71. Palace of the Governors, Uxmal, Yucatán 112
72. Dickinson Residence, sketch 112
73. Dickinson Residence, contemporary view 114
74. Dickinson Residence, steps and terraces 115
75. Dunehouses, early view 118
76. Dunehouses, interior 118
77. Dunehouses, showing orientation 119
78. "The Return of the Cave Man," *Playboy* magazine 123
79. Model of student underground dwelling unit 124
80. Dunehouses, after modifications 125
81. Hilltop House, exterior view 127
82. Hilltop House, model 128
83. Hilltop House, interior, top-floor observatory 129
84. Hilltop House, contemporary view 131
85. Hilltop House, main entrance 132
86. Police Memorial Building, early view 135
87. Police Memorial Building, during construction 136
88. Police Memorial Building, rooftop park 136
89. Police Memorial Building, contemporary view from the south 140
90. Police Memorial Building, north entrance 141
91. Police Memorial Building, rooftop amenities removed 141
92. Pyramid Condominium, drawing 143
93. Pyramid Condominium, model 145
94. Pyramid Condominium, contemporary east-facing view 146
95. Pyramid Condominium, contemporary view from the beach 147
96. Federal Building and Courthouse, Fort Lauderdale 150
97. Federal Building and Courthouse, public areas 151
98. Federal Building and Courthouse, empty fountains 153
99. Daniel State Office Building, Jacksonville 154
100. Daniel State Office Building, riverfront amphitheater 155
101. Daniel State Office Building, exterior 156
102. Daniel State Office Building, interior 157
103. Morgan's notes on Mesoamerican buildings 158
104. Daniel Building as part of Hyatt Regency Riverfront hotel 160
105. William Morgan and family, Copán, Honduras, mid-1970s 162
106. Oceanfront Townhouses, Atlantic Beach 164
107. Naval Submarine Base, Kings Bay, entrance to Fluckey Hall 167

108. Naval Submarine Base, model 168
109. Naval Submarine Base, earthen berms and pyramids 168
110. Grandy Residence, Atlantic Beach, Morgan visiting 170
111. Grandy Residence, elevation 171
112. Grandy Residence, interior 172
113. Grandy Residence, contemporary view 173
114. William Morgan in Micronesia, 1984 175
115. William and Dylan Morgan at the wall tomb of Inol 175
116. U.S. Courthouse, Tallahassee 176
117. Morgan at the University of Florida's Vicenza campus 177
118. Morgan's field notes on earth architecture 178
119. Dylan Morgan House, from beach 179
120. Dylan Morgan House, interior 180
121. Dunehouses, William Morgan House, and Dylan Morgan House 181
122. Lott Residence, Amelia Island 184
123. Lott Residence, section 185
124. Lott Residence, beachside pool area 187
125. Lott Residence, living room and atrium 188
126. Quelch-Gendzier Residence, St. Augustine 191
127. Quelch-Gendzier Residence, drawing 192
128. Quelch-Gendzier Residence, rear, looking southwest 193
129. Quelch-Gendzier Residence, setting for stock photo 194
130. Quelch-Gendzier Residence, inspecting plans 196
131. Quelch-Gendzier Residence, Morgan viewing wetland 196
132. 1942 Beach Avenue, Atlantic Beach, sketch 199
133. 1942 Beach Avenue, section 200
134. Morgan at work, 2015 203

Foreword

The architectural work of William Morgan has been extensively reviewed in the last thirty years. A major book about him by Paul Spreiregen, *The Architecture of William Morgan*, appeared in 1987.[1] It was followed fifteen years later by Robert McCarter's *William Morgan: Selected and Current Works*.[2] These books are the direct predecessors to this new opus on Morgan, fifteen years later again, which reflects not only on the architect's work but on the weaving of his life with his work.

This book reveals to us the universal values that have been a constant in Morgan's life and that have been reflected in his research and his architectural work. The consistency of the ideas and the work, along the whole prolific trajectory of the architect in his lifetime, makes inseparable the research, the writing, and the architectural production set in the development of a man's life. It also reveals to us an architect who reaches the depths of the discipline, nourishing himself from three universal values: the power of built history, comprehension of the human psyche, and a profound understanding of place.

We were not yet talking about resiliency and sustainability in the years when Morgan started interpreting the primitive built environment. These concepts were not included in the academic language, nor were they the focus of disciplinary interest. They certainly were, though, part of the philosophical premises of modern architecture for some of Morgan's Florida modern colleagues. Retroactively, we visualize Morgan as a precursor on the subject, regarding the reach he assigned to its content. He fed on the universal values of timeless architecture and honored them by bringing them into our contemporary culture.

Through Morgan's first four books, we understand the breadth of his research.[3] This original research on ancient civilizations is based on firsthand field documentation of mostly unknown remains of early cultures in North and Central America. The finding and documentation of the prehistoric constructs provided Morgan with primitive though universal principles stemming from age-old understandings of place and climate. His last book, *Earth Architecture: From Ancient to Modern*, makes a comprehensive and didactic contribution to the subject he consistently investigated and directly experienced throughout his whole life.[4] Morgan donated the research materials for his books to the Architecture Archive at the University of Florida Special Collections, and today they constitute an invaluable heritage source, which Shieldhouse draws upon here. From this solid platform, William Morgan's architecture contributions go on to reveal, poetically interpreted, these primeval universal values regarding shelter and dwelling of people on Earth, particularly in this region of the planet.

Ancestral human feelings of shelter are recognized in his work—living on a hilltop dominating the landscape, protected by earth in a cave, or related to the natural elements of the site: the sea, dunes, vegetation, and so on. These are important feelings so threatened in contemporary culture, as are truthful materials, permanence and evolution of the natural surroundings, alliance with the other peoples of the planet, and the plants that shade and shelter us. Behaving with the force of the natural processes, as discussed by Jane Jacobs in *The Nature of Economies*, Morgan's work recognizes the gifts offered to us by the environment, landscape, materials, and climate and takes them to be an integral part of his approach to design—while integrating the accumulated knowledge of our common architectural heritage to reach remarkably forceful contributions to the history of architecture.[5] Certainly, understanding the way his ideas developed across the span of his life allows a much more focused reading of Morgan's work.

Martha Kohen, professor
University of Florida School of Architecture

Introduction

William Newton Morgan was an American architect of singular vision, whose body of work both reflects and transcends the dominant themes of modern architecture—simplicity, lack of ornamentation, and the building as a machine for living.[1] In 1960, as Morgan was beginning his architectural practice, the architect and critic Peter Blake wrote that all modern buildings refer back to Le Corbusier, Mies van der Rohe, or Frank Lloyd Wright.[2] "The fact is that virtually no modern building constructed today would look the way it does if it had not been for the work of one or more of these three men," Blake wrote.[3] There is ample evidence of the influence of Le Corbusier and Wright on Morgan but scant evidence of the curtain walls prevalent in Mies van der Rohe's work. And even though Morgan can be situated in the modernist canon, he did more than amplify the movement's founding voices. As with many highly regarded Florida modernists, Morgan designed buildings that responded to that state's weather. Florida modernists, including Morgan, also made wide use of concrete. With abundant water and sand, concrete was cheap in Florida, and mild winters mean less cracking from the freezing and thawing found in colder climates.

As his career evolved, Morgan transcended the architectural themes of the mid-twentieth century by folding earth architecture and the designs of prehistoric American builders into modernism. The result can be seen in strikingly original government buildings, museums, apartment buildings, and private residences on the East Coast of the United States, particularly in his native state of Florida.

Morgan earned his bachelor's degree in architectural sciences from Harvard College in 1952, with a course of study that initially included pre-law classes and social anthropology, but he later turned toward architecture. Following graduation, he served as an officer in the U.S. Navy in Korea and the Pacific. His military service shaped his design vision by introducing him to the architecture and landscapes of Asian and Pacific civilizations. The navy also instilled in Morgan leadership and focus, both qualities he put to use in his subsequent three years as a married father attending Harvard's Graduate School of Design (GSD) while working part of that time for internationally recognized architect Paul Rudolph, who then maintained an office at 26 Church Street near Harvard Square.

From his earliest assignments at GSD Morgan sought to build upon the architectural foundations of ancient civilizations, reinterpreted for the modern era. He authored five books on archaeology and earth architecture that examine how early civilizations in North America and Micronesia, and elsewhere around the world, adapted buildings to their environments. Morgan's interest in pre-Columbian architecture dates to boyhood summers in the American Southwest, where the arid and less developed desert environment contributed to the survival of numerous pre-Columbian villages.

Although Morgan drew upon early architecture in his designs, his sensibility was fundamentally modern. Morgan trained at one of the key centers of modernism in the world. While at GSD (and as an undergraduate student at Harvard College), he was associated with the modern movement's central figures, such as Josep Lluís Sert and Walter Gropius, as well as with the architectural historian Eduard Sekler. However, the influence of Paul Rudolph on Morgan's work and his approach to design was profound. Rudolph's influences were clearly visible in Morgan's earliest structures in Jacksonville and Atlantic Beach, Florida, and in his searching and creative response to each new commission. There are also numerous parallels between Morgan and his mentor. Both trained at GSD, both served in the navy, both saw their initial professional success in postwar Florida beach communities, both benefited from Harvard's Wheelwright Prize, which exposed them to architecture around the world, and both used modern materials in novel ways that helped to redefine modern architecture.

But while other modernists sought to forge a new architecture by denying the past, Morgan resolutely and increasingly embraced early architecture. In so doing, he made modern forms more meaningful, more approachable, and arguably more intimately linked to the history and essence of the places where they were built.

Morgan described his preference for "fresh, direct, clearheaded designs" and "sensitively related components with consistent details." His approach to each project was simple and bold. His architecture was innovative and daring, and his confidence in his creativity was refreshingly resolute. "The first step in creating architecture is to think outside the box," he said in an interview at eighty-four years of age. "The second step, and those that follow, are the same as the first."

Morgan was a perfectionist, and architects were eager to work for him and learn from him. Most of them later went on to start their own firms. As with many highly respected architects, William Morgan did not lack for ego. One of his last clients, Francis Lott, recalls praising Morgan, who replied: "There is Frank [Lloyd Wright], Mies [van der Rohe], Corbu [Le Corbusier] and *moi*!" But in almost the same breath Morgan could be modest and self-effacing. He delighted in pointing to the lifeguard stand he designed for the City of Atlantic Beach, Florida, and declaring it to be his best work.

This book examines the evolution of Morgan's development as an architect, beginning with the early influences in his childhood and through his undergraduate and graduate studies at Harvard, and continuing to a professional career that spanned the second half of the twentieth century and the early years of the twenty-first. This story is told in words and pictures.

The words—many in the architect's own voice—communicate the spirit of inquiry and invention that characterized Morgan's vision. The accompanying images illustrate and highlight how he translated that vision into a bold corpus of work.

Although much had been written about Morgan, including two architectural monographs, in later years it became evident that there was a need for and the possibility of a book that would be more biographical and personal, one that would consider as well some of his works that had not been documented in the previous monographs. As Morgan stoically battled ailments that limited his activity over the last eight years of his life, the architect, his wife, Bunny, and I all agreed that it would be useful to capture the words and spirit of this creative force. That is the goal of this book. With that goal, most of the information presented on the following pages is derived from personal interviews with Morgan, as well as with his family members, associates, and clients, and from autobiographical notes handwritten by Morgan between 2013 and 2015 and delivered to me.

The objective is not to provide an analysis of Morgan's career, or a comprehensive parade of all his work, but to provide a more personal insight into the forces that shaped a great architect and his achievements.

We begin with a biographical foundation, discussing important events in Morgan's life up to the start of his architectural practice in Atlantic Beach, Florida, near Jacksonville. This includes project examples from Morgan's years at GSD that prefigure major themes of his later work, such as the use of earth as a building material and topography as an element of design, tensile structures to create lightweight and powerful shapes, and tree forms as supports—aspects of his work that developed and evolved as Morgan's career progressed.

The story continues with Morgan's professional career, and it illustrates how the design themes he explored at GSD developed and evolved under his creative watch. For William Newton Morgan, work was very much his life. During much of his career he was in the office six days per week and then worked at home on Sundays. When recessions hit and the architectural practice slowed down, he would turn his focus to archaeological research, which led to the publication of five books on archaeology and architecture during three decades. Morgan was a workaholic, and he constantly thought about architecture, including ancient architecture. As such, a description of his life beyond graduate school should focus on his architecture and his research.

This account relies heavily on Morgan's own recollections and descriptions, but it is not a comprehensive examination of Morgan's work. Rather, it focuses on the core projects that he considered important and relevant to telling the story of his development as an architect. The list of projects selected for highlighting here was developed over the course of many conversations with Morgan in 2014 and 2015.

Two previous works are valuable resources for anyone wanting more information on Morgan. Readers wanting more description of his entire opus and less of a biographical sketch may wish to consult Paul Spreiregen's and Robert McCarter's excellent monographs.[4] This work provides a different perspective by examining the evolution of Morgan's influences and design ideas not only over the course of his long and accomplished career but even further back into his earliest years. I hope it provides added details that supplement the previous monographs.

In recent years many of the buildings designed by modernist architects, who worked principally with concrete, and sometimes in the style described as brutalism, have been demolished or are threatened.[5] As admired as he is by architects, preservationists, and fans of modernism, many of Paul Rudolph's buildings, some of which were concrete fabrications, have been destroyed or disfigured. Since 2007 Riverview High School in Sarasota, Florida, the Orange County Government Center in Goshen, New York, and three private residences have been victimized.

Many of Morgan's larger works arguably fall under the brutalist rubric. But all of Morgan's major commercial, governmental, and religious buildings survive as this is written, although one—the Federal Building and Courthouse in Fort Lauderdale, Florida—faces an uncertain future. Three of his residential projects have been demolished. While some of his remaining works have been adorned or altered in ways that Morgan would find objectionable, the strong and clear statement of his designs remains apparent to an eye educated in his style. Through William Morgan's words and his celebrated structures, this book provides tangible examples of an expressive and individualistic American architect and his contributions to the modern movement.

1

Early Years

William Morgan was born December 14, 1930, to physician Thomas Edward Morgan Sr. and his wife, Kathleen Fiske Morgan. When he was three years of age, the family moved from Jacksonville to Lake City, Florida, some sixty miles away. Thomas Sr. had been a resident physician at the Duval County Hospital in Jacksonville with a specialty in pediatrics. When the Great Depression hit, like many others, he lost his job. In Lake City Morgan's father found work as a general practitioner, but times were tough. Morgan's older brother, Thomas Jr., remembered patients paying their father in fruit and vegetables from their yards and gardens.

Living in Lake City left a deep impression on a young William Morgan. The new home featured a wide front porch and faced a small lake with a sidewalk surrounding it where children often gathered to play. Neighboring one-story houses facing the lake flanked the Morgan home, with a small wide yard between each house and the next. This grouping of houses oriented toward a landscape feature—the lake, and its function as a natural gathering spot for adults and children—Morgan identified as his first experience of place. Early in his childhood at the lakeside home, Morgan came to understand how place creates community. During his architectural career, as he immersed himself in the thinking of early architects, his designs became increasingly sensitive to place, both in their relationship to topography and in Morgan's impulse to create place in designs, such with as the Police Memorial Building and Daniel State Office Building in downtown Jacksonville, and the Florida State Museum (now Dickinson Hall) in Gainesville, where he created places for people to congregate by incorporating rooftop gardens and other gathering spots into the building structure. In doing so, Morgan connected people to these places, to his buildings, and to elements of the landscape that have existed since prehistory.

The communal feeling of living in the lakeside neighborhood, though, was short-lived for the Morgan family. Dr. Morgan advocated vaccines for children starting school, and that ran counter to beliefs of the small, conservative community of Lake City. At the time many conservative Christians believed vaccines interfered with God's will to decide who should be stricken with sickness and who should go unscathed. In their view, Dr. Morgan was interfering with the divine plan. "The two pastors [in town] got together and ran him out of Lake City because he insisted on giving vaccinations against God's will," Morgan's older brother, Thomas, recalled. "My father had a problem. He was interested in childhood diseases."

The loss of a second job during the Great Depression put Dr. Morgan and his family in crisis. He had a wife and two young children to support but no job. A friend in Tallahassee with connections to Florida's state government arranged for him to be hired as the prison doctor at Florida State Prison in Raiford. The family lived on the site of the jail complex in what Thomas described as a three-room shack elevated on cinder blocks, with a tin roof. Thomas remembered the lights in the house dimming whenever a prisoner was electrocuted in Raiford's death chamber.

"I remember playing on dark nights in the winter, and the lights would go dim and my mother would cry because they had just executed someone," Thomas said.

Although he had been run out of Lake City, word of Dr. Morgan's forward-thinking commitment to vaccinating children found its way to the White House. Thomas recalled playing with young William in the front room of their tiny house when a black Buick eased up to the front door. Inside was a well-dressed woman wearing a hat with a large, dramatic brim. "Is this where Dr. Morgan lives?" she asked. Mrs. Morgan told the visitor that her husband was at the prison clinic.

The visitor said she'd heard that there was a doctor in Florida who had gotten in trouble for administering vaccines. She was associated with the Roosevelt Administration and its efforts to bring electrical power to rural areas, and she wanted to meet this doctor. Sometime after that visit, the Roosevelt Administration arranged for Dr. Morgan to receive a fellowship to study at the Harvard School of Public Health.

As the fellowship began in 1935, the family moved into a two-bedroom apartment in Brookline, Massachusetts. Morgan remembered the tall, densely built urban apartment buildings in Brookline. The apartment lacked a yard for young Morgan to play in, so a fire escape outside the tiny living room's window was his fallback option. He recalled spending many hours on that fire escape watching parachutes he fashioned from his father's handkerchiefs drift slowly down into the snow-blanketed alley with no interference from the wind.

Following his graduation from the School of Public Health, Dr. Morgan moved his family back to Florida, where he had been hired to launch a state health department office in the Tampa Bay area. From that job Dr. Morgan was recruited to work for the U.S. Department of Labor by President Franklin Delano Roosevelt's Secretary of Labor Frances Perkins, who was the first woman to serve in a presidential cabinet. The family moved again—this time into a two-story house on a hill in Falls Church, Virginia. Thomas Morgan Jr. recalled Perkins reading children's stories to him and cocktail parties at his family home, with guests such as Roosevelt's Secretary of the Interior Harold Ickes and his Secretary of the Treasury Henry Morgenthau Jr. At the Falls Church home, Morgan's brother also remembered radio and television personality Arthur Godfrey living next to the lot where the Morgan brothers and other neighborhood kids played baseball on Saturdays. "The Old Redhead" would regularly shout at them to curtail their noise.

In 1940 the family returned to northeast Florida and lived in a duplex in Jacksonville's Riverside neighborhood before moving some twenty miles east to Jacksonville Beach.

Figure 1. William Morgan (*left*) and brother, Thomas, on tricycles in Jacksonville's Riverside neighborhood. From the Morgan family.

William Morgan graduated from San Pablo Elementary School in Jacksonville Beach and then from Duncan U. Fletcher High School in Neptune Beach.

The family's first house in Jacksonville Beach was located a block from the Atlantic Ocean, and Morgan noted how its two-story screened-in porch offered a sweeping ocean view. From that high perch, unobstructed by today's high-rise buildings, the beach extended across the horizon in both directions. Later, as an architect, Morgan was sensitive to the need to preserve water views.

Morgan's family moved frequently, following the demands of his father's career, but he recalled those moves as educational. By the time Morgan graduated from high school, the family had lived in ten different homes in ten different settings. In addition to the house by the lake and the multi-story apartment building, he had lived in a garage apartment in Augusta, Georgia; a simple one-story in a suburban neighborhood in Clearwater, Florida; a house with an ocean view; and the two-story house on top of a hill in Falls Church, Virginia. Reflecting later, Morgan said the experience of living in so many different settings profoundly influenced his sense of how building design and landscapes shape people, family life, and neighborhoods.

When the United States entered World War II after the bombing of Pearl Harbor on December 7, 1941, Dr. Morgan was drafted into the U.S. Army. He was stationed in Las Vegas, Nevada, where he held the rank of major and was appointed the military governor of the military district of southern Nevada, Thomas said. As part of his duties, he created a health clinic for the Clark County Health Department. There were plenty of patients. The military had undertaken a massive training program in Las Vegas, preparing soldiers and airmen to operate B-17 and B-24 bombers. There were Native Americans in the region, workers building the Hoover Dam, and prostitutes who had been brought in by the mob, Thomas said, to serve the burgeoning military population.

For three summers William and Thomas lived with their father in Las Vegas, visiting the Grand Canyon, Yosemite, Zion National Park, Bryce Canyon National Park, and other places

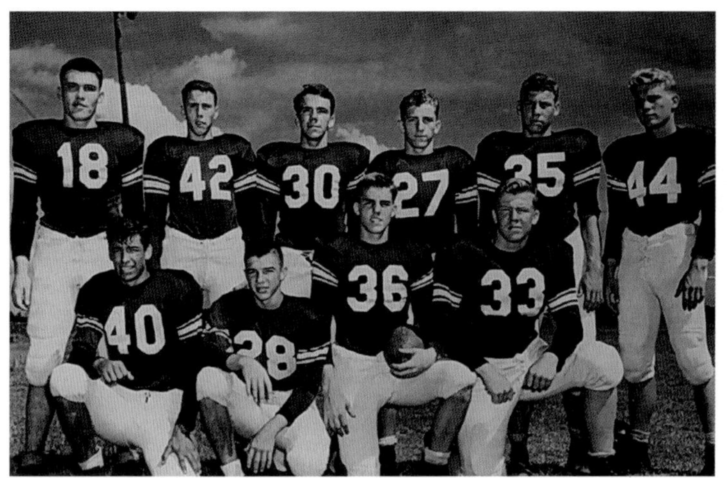

Far left: Figure 2. Morgan (#33) with Duncan U. Fletcher High School teammates. From the Morgan family.

Left: Figure 3. High school portrait of Morgan. From the Morgan family.

that are less well known. William Morgan's interest in archaeology dates to these explorations of sites where pre-Columbian peoples lived. "I grew up in a modern Pueblo Indian community and spent much time within and around the ruins of the Pajarito Plateau of northern New Mexico," the architect wrote in the foreword to one of his archaeological studies.[1] On the southern rim of the Grand Canyon, the brothers visited a little-known pre-Columbian site featuring remains of a ball court that resembled the grand ball court of the Mayan site Chichén Itzá, his brother, Thomas, recalled.

Back in Jacksonville Beach for the school year, Morgan played the snare drum in the Fletcher High School marching band and joined the Latin Club, following his brother's lead. He played football, becoming the team's co-captain, and edited the school's yearbook during his senior year.

The Morgan brothers scrambled for money, like other teenagers. They delivered newspapers, but their biggest and most lucrative venture was hauling out cars stuck in beach sand. The brothers drove a black 1928 Model A convertible with yellow rims. They dubbed it the

"Yellow Peril" and drove seven miles up and down the beach, from Ponte Vedra to Atlantic Beach, looking for customers. Thomas had bought the car with seventy-five dollars earned from his paper route. When his older brother left for college, William inherited the Yellow Peril and ran the "Morgan Rescue Service" with a friend, Thomas recalled. Morgan fastened to the car a makeshift sign reading "Pullouts $25," which he would stash when police were nearby.

2

Harvard College

After graduation from Fletcher High School, Thomas entered Duke University to pursue a medical career, following in his father's footsteps. William's career path, however, remained uncertain. Harvard wanted students to obtain a broad-based introduction in the liberal arts and then to dive deeply into a particular area of concentration. Although he won a four-year navy ROTC scholarship to Harvard, Morgan did not decide upon a concentration until he was a junior.

Morgan had previously assumed that he would follow his brother and his father into a career in medicine. But a fishing trip in Las Vegas with the pair convinced Morgan he did not have a passion for that vocation. After a day of fishing on Lake Mead, Morgan watched Thomas and his father clean strings of bass and crappie, which they then threw into a pile of dry ice before skinning. As they removed the organs and tossed them into the water, the pair noted how one could tell where a fish had been by the food in its gut, and they then proceeded to list the fishes' various organs and talk about how they fit together. They were enthralled by all this. Morgan was not. "It didn't turn me on," he said.

If he wasn't going to be a doctor, Morgan settled on what he then perceived to be the next best thing—he would pursue a career in the law. But the law did not suit his temperament either. Morgan had taken several government courses that were relevant to a pre-law curriculum, and it soon became evident that he had neither the aptitude for nor an interest in that field of study. Morgan also acquired numerous credits in social anthropology. This foundation would contribute mightily to shaping his interest in early builders and eventually to his unique blend of early architecture and modernism.

Harvard has a series of residential houses, which provide a rich intellectual and social experience, in addition to their functions as places to eat and sleep. The stimulating life in Lowell House had a profound impact on the undergraduate from Florida. "Lowell House was for me the most critical part of the education at Harvard," Morgan said, "because you met there all these distinguished scholars with whom you would have dinner and discuss things. I learned more in Lowell House than anywhere else. There and in Jim Cronin's beer emporium.[1] John F. Kennedy was also a Lowell House man."

Morgan said listening to a Lowell House advisor's stories about studying a group of indigenous South Africans fascinated him and prompted him to take courses in anthropology. "I remember one of the fellows was doing work in South Africa with a particular group of Africans. He was studying the habits and so forth. I was enthralled and would sit for hours in the Lowell House dining hall, listening to him talk about his work in Africa." Morgan was also influenced by a friendship with Edgar F. Shannon, whose field was English and who later became president of the University of Virginia.

Reflecting on his interest in ancient cultures, Morgan saw a natural link between architecture and prehistoric cultures and their artifacts—anthropology and archaeology. "Archaeology and architecture are very closely intertwined. It's very difficult to separate them, particularly in the case of an introductory course, which is what I had: an introduction to various peoples and their habits and the world that they shaped for themselves," he remembered. "It was just a matter of looking at the people and what they were doing, in the way of housing, and group housing, their villages and what they did to make it possible to live there in very adverse conditions. What a wonderful combination of events—all tied up to make those civilizations! I just thought that was the most interesting stuff, by far more interesting than anything else I could think of."

However, by his junior year, Morgan had changed his concentration three times—from government to philosophy to anthropology. The stimulating environment at Harvard College may have rendered Morgan's choice of a concentration more difficult. He had many interests, and he was unsure what career best suited him. He realized then that he would have to pick a concentration and stick with it.

Morgan finally settled upon architecture as a field of study when Dean William Bender stopped him as he was crossing Harvard Yard one day during his junior year. Bender had recently learned that Morgan had changed his major for a third time, and he was concerned. "Morgan, come here," Dean Bender called out, according to Morgan's recollection. "What's this nonsense about changing your major again?" He asked the Harvard junior just how long he thought it would take for him to graduate. Morgan replied that he had a deadline. He had to finish in four years or by the time his scholarship expired. Bender said he would never make it unless he chose a concentration and stuck with it. Morgan was interested in too many subjects, the dean opined, and he ordered Morgan to follow him into his office.

"We went into his office and he got out these books and started looking," Morgan remembered, "and he said, 'Here's one . . . architecture! You can major in architecture.' This was in 1950—my junior year." Morgan realized Dean Bender had decided his concentration for him. He acquiesced, and Bender seemed pleased.

"Fine," said Bender, pointing to a building outside the office window. "Architecture meets in that building right over there."

Morgan's letters home to his mother indicate that Bender's suggestion was a success. In one letter he reflected on a jury selecting one of his earliest architectural designs:

> I guess the greatest thing that has happened in a long time is about my school. It is a very wonderful feeling for me to have presented my idea, thoroughly convinced that it

> was as boldly imaginative and as economical and practical as the requirements demanded.

Other undergraduate projects included a roadside farm stand and a sling chair. The farm stand was "designed to express the honest character of the hard-working New England farmer. The materials were native stone and timber; the structure fairly simple, but strongly organized and rugged—just as the farmer himself must be to carve a living from the rocky New England soil."

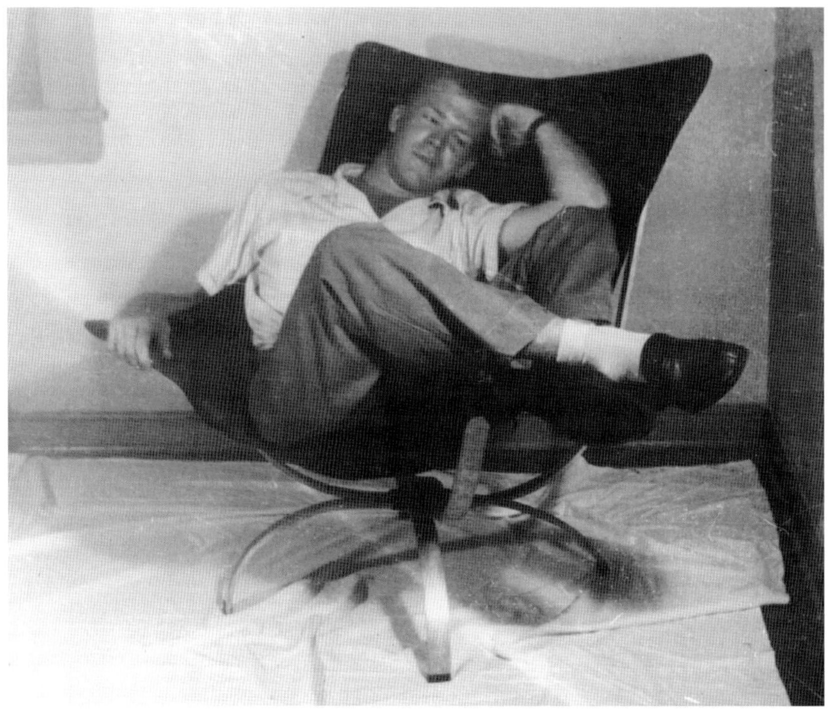

Figure 4. William Morgan demonstrating his patented design for a sling chair. From the Morgan family.

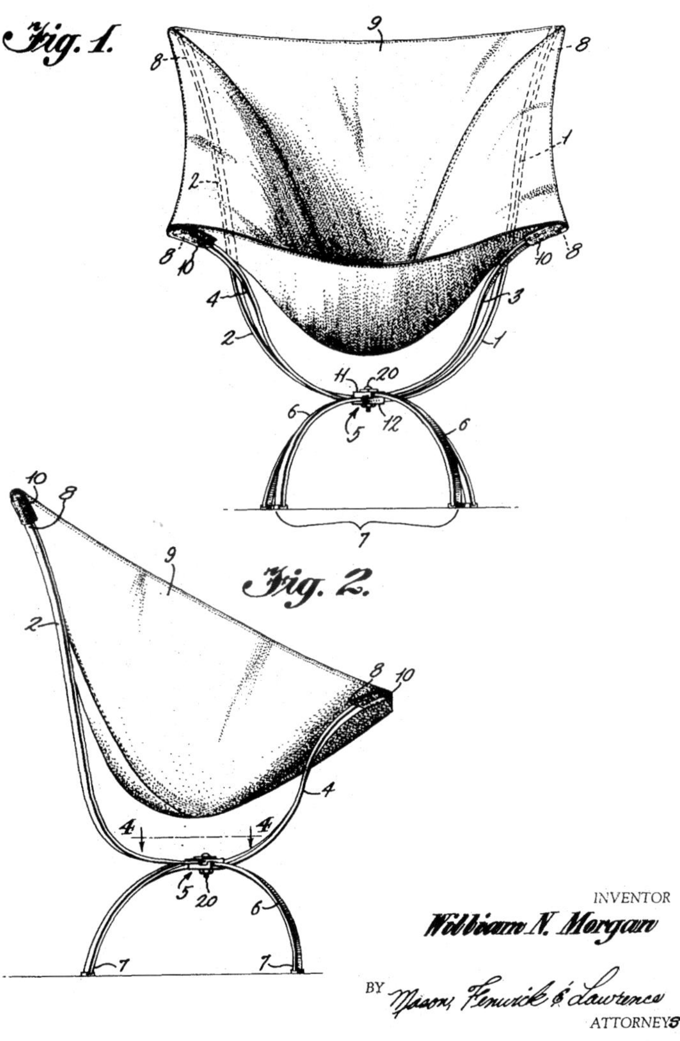

Figure 5. Patent US 2,689,602, "sling-type chair." Source: U.S. Patent and Trademark Office.

Figure 6. Morgan during a summer cruise as part of his Naval ROTC training. The name "W. M. Morgan" was incorrectly stenciled on his jumper. From the Morgan family.

The sling chair was supported by four intersecting polished metal rungs that meet under the seat. Two of the rungs fan out to create the chair's base, while the other two support the back of the sling. Morgan received a patent, US2689602 A, for this undergraduate project on September 21, 1954. Later, during his professional career, he designed a simple and durable teak chair, which he had manufactured in Indonesia and sold in limited quantities.

The ROTC scholarship imposed additional requirements on Morgan. During the summer of 1949 he sailed on the battleship *Missouri* to Cherbourg and visited Mont Saint-Michel, Chartres, and Paris. It was the first of many trips overseas.

3

Navy Service

Morgan joined the U.S. Navy immediately after receiving his artium baccalaureus (A.B.) degree with a concentration in architectural sciences from Harvard College in 1952. He was commissioned as an ensign and assigned to the destroyer USS *Bausell*, then operating in Korean waters. He served as the ship's operations officer, air traffic control officer, and legal officer, Morgan said, until he transferred to the admiral's staff on Guam.

While in the Pacific, Morgan took advantage of a few days of onshore leave during his first year to visit Frank Lloyd Wright's Imperial Hotel. When the USS *Bausell* docked in the Japanese city of Yokosuka for several days of servicing, Morgan caught an express train to Tokyo. He described his overnight stay at Wright's Imperial Hotel as one of the great pleasures of his time in the Pacific region.

Architectural historian Sigfried Giedion once observed: "The Japanese house impressed Frank Lloyd Wright as a 'supreme study in elimination—not only of dirt, but the elimination, too, of the insignificant.'"[1] Wright revered Japanese design, and his design included the aesthetics of Japanese cultural traditions reinterpreted by early modernist sensibility. Architectural critic Peter Blake noted the Imperial Hotel's resemblance to Mayan temples. Blake believed Wright tried to bring "something beautiful of the Western Hemisphere to the Japanese Islands."[2]

Figure 7. Lieutenant (junior grade) W. N. Morgan, on duty in the Pacific. From the Morgan family.

Morgan was deeply moved by the building and Wright's interpretation of Japanese design principles. Of the experience, he recounted: "The taxi arrived in the hotel's forecourt, an appropriate entry near the middle of the three-story building complex. Checking in was a regal experience for the hotel's guests—sculpted columns, carpet inlaid with polished stone, a relatively low ceiling, and indirect lighting imparted a feeling of unhurried opulence."

Rather than rushing to his room after checking in, Morgan strolled through the lobby and seated himself in one of several small reception areas, ordered a nightcap, and watched the guests coming and going. When he went to his room for the night, Morgan noted that it was furnished with great restraint, a characteristic of Japanese design. Waking the next morning, he looked out on a garden scene through the high windows on one side of his room.

"Something like vertical pipes covered with feathers were constantly and gracefully moving back and forth in view," he remembered. "When I arose, I discovered that my high windowsill was at the central garden's level; the 'pipes' that I observed were actually the necks of graceful swans gliding across the central garden's ponds," he said.

Looking back, Morgan considered himself lucky to have had this experience: "I was fortunate to see the original Imperial Hotel. Although it survived a severe earthquake and World War II, the original hotel has been razed, and a new high-rise likewise named 'Imperial Hotel' has been erected. Gone forever are the beauty and elegance of the original complex."[3]

Morgan was also moved by Japanese culture. "Theirs is a wonderful heritage," he wrote home in 1953. "I saw an architecture I hardly knew existed and learned to understand it—a worthwhile experience for me."

In addition to enabling him to see Wright's hotel firsthand, the navy gave Morgan an opportunity to experience the native culture and architectural artifacts of a preindustrial society. In Guam Morgan observed how the dwellings of the native Chamorro people responded to the hot, humid tropical climate. He saw the remnants of the early Chamorro housing using a "group of columns and capstones that together comprise a single foundational structure"—the *latte* set—which formed the base for raised dwellings with steep thatched roofs.[4] He also saw many examples of typical island homes built by native peoples in the Pacific islands where the roofs provided shade and protection from the elements, and large openings allowed for cross-ventilation. When Morgan entered Harvard's Graduate School of Design after his military service, his first design project was the lightweight and portable Guam Vacation House, which was inspired by these dwellings.

It was on Guam that William met and married Bernice "Bunny" Leimback. She was an art teacher in the local high school, teaching native students and U.S. dependents to draw and paint.

A native of Michigan, Bunny graduated from Michigan State University in 1950 and spent three years in Muskegon Heights and Jackson, first as a junior high school teacher and later as an elementary art supervisor. In the latter role she would visit various classrooms at all grades to provide guidance to teachers on art instruction as well as teaching art herself.

Bunny was frustrated with the long, cold winters in Michigan. She thought the climate of the tropics would suit her better and was eager to move. She applied for positions in the Virgin Islands, the Panama Canal Zone, and Hawaii. Later, one of the teachers she supervised told her about a position in Guam. Bunny applied and was accepted. She taught in Guam for two years, with her marriage to William occurring after the first year.

The couple took advantage of leave time for a honeymoon that included visits to the region's architectural and archaeological sites and to Japan. On the island of Tinian north of Guam in the Mariana Islands, the Morgans visited the House of Taga, which Morgan later documented in his book *Prehistoric Architecture in Micronesia*.[5]

Morgan's naval experience also provided him with his first encounter with a "starchitect." Shortly after Morgan's arrival on Guam, Admiral Marion E. Murphy called the young man into his office. The admiral told Morgan to receive the architect Richard Neutra and his wife when they landed at Guam's civilian airport. He instructed Morgan to treat the Neutras with

Above: Figure 8. Bunny and William Morgan at their engagement party in Guam, 1954. From the Morgan family.

Right: Figure 9. The wedding of Bunny and William Morgan, Guam, 1954. From the Morgan family.

respect and allow them to rest for as long as they wanted, but Morgan was also ordered to restrict them to the confines of the tiny civilian airport facilities. They were forbidden to leave the area, Admiral Murphy ordered.

The U.S. government had hired Neutra's firm to develop a master plan for the war-ravaged island—an architect's dream job. Neutra and partner Robert Alexander prepared the master plan, which included the governor's house, an elementary school, and the Guam legislature building. But many of the projects were scuttled with the arrival of a newly appointed, more conservative Guamanian governor in 1953.[6] According to Morgan, Neutra's architectural firm, Neutra and Alexander, had brought a lawsuit against the U.S. government to recover costs from the design and working drawings for the island's building projects.

When the plane arrived, a visibly upset Neutra strode down the stairway holding a copy of *Time* magazine with his own face splashed across the cover. When Morgan explained the limits of his confinement, Neutra became indignant. But Morgan had anticipated his anger. Before the architect's arrival, Morgan canvassed the island, carefully photographing Neutra's work. He assembled the photographs into a catalogue of 35-millimeter transparencies and presented it to the noted architect. Morgan remembered the designs as far ahead of their time. He particularly admired the Francisco Q. Sanchez Elementary School, with its white concrete flat slabs cantilevered from a green tropical hillside, extensive overhangs with open walls instead of window glazing, and courtyards for improved air circulation.[7] "Neutra's work was on the cutting edge of modern architecture," Morgan said.

One of Morgan's most prominent memories of his time in the navy involved a visit by the USS *Bausell* to Hong Kong, where he would decline an opportunity to become a defector and spy for the Chinese.

During the summer of 1953, the *Bausell*'s sagging morale was relieved by a brief visit to Hong Kong, then a British colony on the coast of mainland China. The Communist takeover of the mainland was in full swing.

I arranged to spend a day at Repulse Bay, where sandy beaches, sunbathing, and surfing were said to be the main attractions. Another officer from our wardroom joined me. We changed our clothes in one of the bathhouses along the beach and proceeded to plunge into the gentle surf. My attention was drawn to a yacht anchored in the middle of the bay. I decided to swim out and have a closer look at what appeared to be bathing beauties splashing and diving in the clear water. My fellow officer was not a strong swimmer; he declined my invitation to swim out to the yacht.

As I neared my objective, the bathing beauties greeted me, the only male in the water. I was tired after my long swim, and gratefully appreciated their warm invitation to board the yacht. I had a drink, or two, by way of catching up. The yacht was evidently a former naval vessel about the size of a patrol torpedo boat (PT), which had been converted thoughtfully into a civilian party boat. Two of the men aboard were very interested in me and my work aboard the *Bausell*: radios, radar, air traffic control, sonar, code encryption and decryption, ship types and numbers available, and other information that I was not inclined to divulge.

My hosts needed my information in their work, it seemed. They were reluctant to discuss exactly what they did for a living. Although I had consumed several of their drinks, I had the distinct impression that my hosts' activities were not compatible with those of my ship. They described living in China in glowing terms and suggested that I would find their line of work there highly lucrative. The more they talked, the more out of place I felt. I sensed the faint vibration of engines starting and decided to leave my hosts while I could. When the yacht's bow came about and headed for the mouth of the bay, I stepped out of the cabin, climbed up on the closest railing, and jumped as far as I could in order to miss the churning propellers. As I became airborne, the yacht's engine roared up to flank speed and it headed past the jetty and into the open sea.

I looked around; the evening was descending on Repulse Bay. I reckoned that the closest shore was near the jetty's mouth. I swam for the beach and then began to hike toward the bathhouse, about two miles away around the shoreline. In pitch darkness, I arrived at the bathhouse. It was closed. I found a side entry and proceeded to my locker, dressed, and hired a taxi to take me to my ship's landing. The last liberty boat returned me to the *Bausell*. The ship was getting underway for another deployment on the China Patrol. I felt I had made the right decision when I declined the opportunity to reside in China.

4

Harvard Graduate School of Design

After three years in the western Pacific, Morgan left the U.S. Navy and returned in 1955 to Harvard, where he entered the Graduate School of Design in pursuit of a master's degree in architecture. The young couple rented an apartment in a three-story building at 7 Sumner Road in Cambridge, not far from the drafting room in Harvard Yard. Bunny supplemented the couple's savings and William's GI Bill benefits by teaching in the public schools of Brookline and in summer school at Beaver Country Day School in Newton.

It was a stressful time for the couple. Graduate architecture students spend massive amounts of time working in the studio, and Morgan—a perfectionist—was no exception. Simultaneously, Bunny was busy commuting to her teaching job. After their first son was born, the couple found it easy to hire a competent babysitter, which enabled her to resume teaching four months after their son's birth.

Paul Rudolph's Office

Shortly after his return to Cambridge in 1955 Morgan visited the tiny third-floor Church Street offices of architect Paul Rudolph to ask for a job. Morgan said he had one goal upon returning from the Far East: to work with Rudolph. At the peak of his career, Rudolph's name was grouped with the most exalted names in the profession, including Eero Saarinen, Louis Kahn, Philip Johnson, Pietro Belluschi, Minoru Yamasaki, and I. M. Pei.[1] Morgan knew Rudolph had just won a commission to design the Jewett Art Center at Wellesley College, and he hoped the noted architect might need help.[2]

Figure 10. Architecture student at Harvard's Graduate School of Design, 1957. From the Morgan family.

"I went to see him one day—I think it was a Saturday—everyone else was elsewhere, and Paul was there," Morgan recalled. "I introduced myself and came to the point—I was looking for some kind of apprenticeship employment." Rudolph was blunt in his response. Unless Morgan knew how draw or draft, and could produce ink perspective drawings, he would be worthless. But Morgan was undeterred. He asked Rudolph if he could look around the office. He described Rudolph as then hiding behind a hanging partition while Morgan took in the messy maelstrom of Rudolph's creativity. "There were a number of plywood flush doors on wooden sawhorses and some Luxo lamps that I think must have been left over from the First World War," said Morgan. "It was really a mess. But I found a broom, and I started sweeping the office. I started the one side, sweeping to the other, and then picking up all these pieces of paper, drawings, and things off the floor." When he was done, Rudolph relented and permitted Morgan to stay.

"You can hang around," the taciturn architect offered.

"So I did," said Morgan. "And that was the beginning of really learning about architecture. I am forever in debt to Paul for that experience."

In addition to his demanding studies and studio work at the Graduate School of Design, Morgan had become Paul Rudolph's only student employee. Morgan learned from his mentor, and Rudolph's influence can be seen in the honesty of Morgan's work, its expressiveness, and the ceaseless creativity that enlivened even the architect's most mundane assignments. An observer familiar with Rudolph's beautiful and precise ink drawings will see this skill and technique reflected in Morgan's own draftsmanship.

Rudolph's career began after World War II in Sarasota, Florida, where his lightweight and airy designs for houses and schools, often using innovative materials, attracted international attention. With a commission to design the Mary Cooper Jewett Art Center at Wellesley College in Massachusetts, he established the office near Harvard Square in Cambridge.[3] "The place where I learned something about the practice of architecture and the creation of it was in the office of Paul Rudolph," Morgan said.

In Rudolph's office Morgan worked for an architect who pushed himself and his staff to bring his prodigious ideas to reality. "An idea came up in the morning and was incorporated in two dimensions that night for a meeting with a client," Morgan recalled.

Although Rudolph was driven, his approach was always characterized by freshness and creativity. "I never saw him repeat the features of one project for another client," Morgan said. "He never did a single thing twice."

Rudolph's knowledge of materials gave him latitude in design, but he always celebrated the integrity of whichever medium he chose. That impressed Morgan. "Paul knew steel and glass backwards and forwards. He knew what it could do and what it could not do; it talked to him and he talked to it. He was extremely alert to the potentials of this material," Morgan said. "One thing that was important to Paul was consistency in material. If you start out using steel, you stick with steel; you don't make it look like wood or something else."

Morgan's employment with Rudolph provided exposure to a significant force in American architecture—at its peak. The respect given to Rudolph by visiting luminaries cast its halo on Morgan, then a first-year graduate student in architecture, and enhanced his standing at the GSD.

"By any measure he was one of the finest U.S. architects—as a matter of fact, world architects—of the twentieth century," Morgan asserted. (Rudolph went on to become chair of the architecture program at Yale University in 1958.) Under Rudolph's tutelage Morgan quickly learned the drafting and drawing skills that his mentor needed. He learned how to draw infill shadows, put in trees, render skies, and eventually draw the buildings themselves. He worked on several drawings for the Jewett Art Center and the additions Rudolph designed for Sarasota High School. Some of his drawings appeared in *Architectural Record* after the project was completed.

At Rudolph's office Morgan also learned the importance of connections, and he made plenty himself, in a setting both more personal and more professional than that of the Graduate School of Design. From Rudolph he learned the importance of meeting people from around the world and traveling to other places to view buildings and environments firsthand. Because of Rudolph's reputation, architects traveling to Boston frequently asked to meet with the luminary at his Cambridge office. Consequently, as part of Rudolph's team, Morgan had the opportunity to engage with some of the leading architects of the day.

The people who worked with Morgan and who visited his office were the architects whose ideas, whose designs, and whose projects were featured in *Architectural Record*, *Progressive Architecture,* and other leading design periodicals. It was a heady experience to be among them. "These were the guys who were doing it. They were making America's architecture," Morgan said. "They were really grinding out what we would see next week or next month in any edition of whatever magazine you might see. That's who those guys were."

Morgan recalled that he and Rudolph were working late one night when the Russian-born architect and academic Serge Chermayeff knocked on the door. Chermayeff taught at the GSD and became head of its Department of Architecture in 1953.[4] Morgan described Chermayeff as "a distinguished, tall, and thoughtful man who offered cutting remarks that made little pieces out of pompous asses." In addition to his academic work, Chermayeff was a practicing architect. He designed a number of vacation houses on Cape Cod noted for their strong modernist lines, soaring interior spaces, and use of geometric patterns painted in bold primary colors on exterior panels. They stood out from the typical clapboard cottages that dominated the coast.

Chermayeff had brought some drawings with him, and he asked Morgan for a critique.

Morgan was stunned. "This can't be right," he remembered thinking. "I can't be the student having the gall to critique such a distinguished, internationally famous designer as Serge Chermayeff . . . but I did."

A visit from architect Joseph Zalewski provided Morgan insight into the minds of two creative geniuses pushing each other to greater creative heights. Zalewski had worked in the studio of Le Corbusier, and Morgan considered him one of the finest professors teaching at the Graduate School of Design. Learning that Morgan was employed by Rudolph, Zalewski asked him to arrange an introduction. One Saturday afternoon not long afterward, Zalewski knocked on the Church Street office door. Morgan recalled the display of brilliance that followed:

> As usual, Paul and I were the only people working. Paul was working on the south elevation of the new Sarasota High School. He was deeply absorbed in the aesthetics of the elevation. He was working with sun shades and articulation of shadow in a very forceful, very dynamic way. Rudolph and Zalewski nodded to each other and may have said "hello," but they never exchanged another word during their entire meeting. Paul had sketched out the entire façade of the conceptual south elevation of the high school. Zalewski took one look at Paul's drawing, and he rolled out yellow tracing paper over it and then made a gesture for Paul to stand aside. Paul did so, just looking at him bug-eyed. Zalewski took his pencil and drew the entire south elevation, every shadow. It was a very dynamic, very strong drawing, but it was not the building that Paul had drawn. Zalewski had completely rethought Paul's design. Paul then made a motion for Zalewski to step aside, and Paul rolled a third sheet of paper over the previous two designs, and he proceeded to draw a completely new version of the building, with emphasis where he intended it to be. When he stepped back from that, Zalewski stepped up and gestured so as to indicate: "This wouldn't do; it's not right." He then drew another completely new version. I was just amazed. These guys knew exactly what they

were drawing, and they were making references to principles and ideas—not nitpicking about details.

When Morgan left the office for the evening, the pair of veteran architects were still engaged in their wordless discussion. "That's the way real architects are. They don't talk about baloney, and they don't read baloney books, but they draw," Morgan said. "They look at each other's work, and they exchange ideas just through the hands."

As Morgan understood the inner workings of the office better, Rudolph relied on him more and more to pay bills and make sure the day-to-day affairs were taken care of. Rudolph had a reputation for absent-mindedness, and he trusted Morgan to keep his books straight.

"There was an open book and blank checks. As needed, I would write checks for outstanding expenses," Morgan recalled. "One time, Paul said: 'Just keep an account of your hours and write yourself a check for your amount.'" Rudolph apparently had forgotten that Morgan was merely an unpaid apprentice. He told Morgan to make sure that the telephone bills and the lights were paid, and, of course, to cut a check for his own salary.

"I said, 'But Paul, I'm not getting any pay.' And he replied: 'Why don't you just put down whatever you think is right, and pay yourself every week?' So I did." Morgan paid himself less than any of the more experienced staff, reluctant to value his own contributions at the same level as those of people he believed knew far better how to put together a building. "They knew what a foundation was, what a setback was, and all kinds of phrases that either meant absolutely nothing to me or were only very obscure ideas," Morgan explained." Morgan was learning all these things and would soon put them to good use.

Rudolph's unpredictable personality, poor office management, and volatility have all been documented, but Morgan made himself indispensable.[5] He saw Rudolph's famous temper, but the star architect never lashed out at the young apprentice.

Once, when Rudolph was working on the Jewett Art Center, Morgan helped produce a rendering for publication in *Architectural Record*. Rudolph looked at Morgan's drawing and instructed him to put shading in the background, which would contrast with the building in the foreground. Rudolph picked up a sheet of dotted halftone Zip-A-Tone (an adhesive drafting product for adding shading and texture) and handed it to Morgan for the background. "I added the Zip-A-Tone to portions that represented the sky, which was interlaced with trees and the Wellesley campus," Morgan explained. "The filigree of those Gothic buildings at Wellesley was very delicate. The rendering was more or less complete by two or three in the morning. When I got Paul to look at it, I removed the Zip-A-Tone . . . and the background completely disappeared with it." Rudolph was not happy. "His face turned all colors of red," Morgan recalled. "He didn't say anything. He went out to the stairs—thump, thump, thump—then up the stairs, to a place where there was some water—a lavatory." Rudolph wet some paper towels and wadded them up. He came back into the office mopping the back of his neck. "I think if there had been fire coming out of his ears, I wouldn't have been surprised," observed Morgan. Instead of exploding at his inexperienced charge, Rudolph called the editor of *Architectural Record* and secured a two-day delay, holding a spot in the magazine for the illustration.

Witnessing Rudolph's creative intellect inspired Morgan to take risks and to design buildings of his own that pushed the edges of the possible and that spoke to him artistically and intellectually. Morgan, however, admitted to being so awestruck by Rudolph's accomplishments that he never showed his mentor any of his student designs. He also remembered making an effort to keep Rudolph from realizing just how little he knew about the practice of architecture. "I didn't have the temerity to show Paul anything I had ever drawn, other than some very pedestrian things," he said, "but it was watching the real architects in the office—what they were doing—talking with them, and having lunch with them—that helped me to learn. I asked them to show me what to do because I was so embarrassed, and I didn't want to demonstrate my ignorance to Paul any more than I really had to."

While reflecting on his time in Rudolph's office, Morgan recalled the architect providing pragmatic tips on how to keep a client's point of view from destroying a good design. For a home in Brookline commissioned by a Mr. and Mrs. Yanofsky, Morgan prepared the schematics in a pinwheel plan to show to the clients. They said yes to everything. When preparing the final design, Rudolph instructed Morgan to move the refrigerator to the middle of the kitchen:

> Pointing to the drawing, Paul said: "Erase the refrigerator and put it over here." Put it in the middle of the kitchen? I asked. He said, "That's right, put it in the middle of the kitchen." Why would you put it in the middle of the kitchen? "You know, clients always like to change something, so give them something that we can agree on," Paul replied. Sure enough, when Mrs. Yanofsky looked over the plans, she said the refrigerator was in the wrong location, just as Rudolph had predicted. Paul said, "That's brilliant, Mrs. Yanofsky." The Yanofskys didn't touch anything else. That was enough.

On several occasions during his professional career, Morgan included sunken living rooms in his designs, a feature that at times was rejected by otherwise compliant clients. One might speculate that these sunken living rooms functioned as Morgan's own equivalent to Rudolph's out-of-place refrigerator.

One of the most entertaining architects to parade through Rudolph's Church Street office was Philip Johnson. Known for his outsized personality and outlandish stories, Johnson enthralled Morgan. Later in Morgan's career the connection proved professionally beneficial. Johnson's connections with the MIT press helped facilitate the 1980 publication of Morgan's first book, *Prehistoric Architecture in the Eastern United States*. Johnson also was instrumental in Morgan getting his first commission to design a department store. He recalled:

> During a large AIA reception in Washington, Philip thanked me for a minor favor I had done for him while I was the chairman of the National AIA Committee of Design.[6] Philip wanted me to meet someone across the noisy, crowded hall. He stopped abruptly and slapped a very big, bald-headed man on the back. It was Stanley Marcus

of Neiman Marcus fame. Philip asked, "Stanley, did you ever build that little store in Florida?"

Marcus answered, "No, but we expect to soon."

Philip replied, "I'd like you to meet the finest architect in Florida, Bill Morgan."

We shook hands and Stanley asked, "Where is your office, Bill?"

Before I could answer, Philip interrupted. "Where is the store, Stanley?"

"Fort Lauderdale," said Stanley.

"That's where Bill's office is!" Philip interjected. My office was actually in Jacksonville, three hundred miles away. The truth notwithstanding, I designed the Fort Lauderdale store, which led to designing a Bloomingdale's store in Miami.

Whenever Johnson visited Boston, everyone in Rudolph's office would go out to lunch with him, where he regaled them with stories. "He was not in Paul's league as an architect, but he was a remarkable character," said Morgan, "and Paul had a great respect for Philip."

Morgan remembered lunching alone with Johnson at Young Lee Chinese restaurant, across the street from the Church Street office.[7] The pair entered the restaurant at noon and didn't depart until 5:00 p.m. During the long lunch Johnson spoke about his ideas for the design of the Seagram building in Manhattan, for which Johnson collaborated with Mies van der Rohe. He wanted to build two ponds with fountains in the entryway of a formal plaza, but Manhattan's taxi drivers objected. It was a good spot for picking up fares, and the spray from the fountains would soak their customers. Johnson explained to Morgan that he wanted a mist of vodka and gin spraying from the fountains in front of the U.S. headquarters of the Canadian distillery, not water. "He was serious!" Morgan said. "He tried to tell the client that a vodka or gin mist from the fountains would not have an adverse effect." Johnson claimed to have arranged for MIT to make test basins to develop a means of controlling the spray.

"He had one after another of these outrageous adventures," Morgan said. "He would lead you on to completely believing all this stuff, and then he'd abruptly leave the restaurant, letting you decide whether or not he was serious. Philip never pretended to be a great designer," Morgan added, "but he was a very great connoisseur of architecture and he fortunately had enough money to keep him afloat in the wonderful world of Oz that he surrounded himself with."

Ultimately, the challenges of working for Paul Rudolph, often into the early hours of the morning, while simultaneously carrying the demanding workload of a graduate student in architecture, proved unworkable. After eight or nine months of working for Rudolph and attending classes at the GSD, Morgan realized he was in trouble. When Rudolph needed a project completed, nobody did anything else until it was done. His professors at the GSD also realized he couldn't manage both. "The school people finally said, 'Enough is enough. Either you work for him or you withdraw from school,'" Morgan recalled.

Morgan also wondered if the ultimatum from GSD wasn't an attempt to get rid of a troublemaker. Morgan may not have shown his work to Rudolph, but he brought ideas from Rudolph's office into the GSD, pushed himself to create his own individualistic designs, and began to question openly the relevance of the GSD curriculum. "I was dragging a whole lot of ideas into the studios that they didn't want to hear," he said. "I was much too adventurous and much too experimental and much too advanced. They were looking for the meat and potatoes that the students could understand and go out and build something with, and what I was talking about was on the Moon. It was way out there. They didn't need any more of Morgan's wild ideas." In the winter of 1956 Morgan resigned from Rudolph's office and focused on completing the GSD program, which was interrupted only by a 1957 summer internship at Smith, Hinchman and Grylls in Detroit.

GSD Experiences

As a way to know and to assess individual students, the GSD faculty assigned members of Morgan's new class a weekend problem during the fall of 1955—design a vacation house. The retreat could be of any type and anywhere in the world. Having recently returned from a year and a half on Guam during his navy service, Morgan chose a remote site on the island's rugged northeast coast for his vacation house. The site was situated on a narrow shelf of land at the base of sheer cliffs.

Morgan drew the design on a 22-by-28-inch sheet of Strathmore paper depicting a clearing in the jungle with an erected tent consisting of eight-foot-square fabric panels stiffened by aluminum "X" braces and attached to one another with continuous zippers along adjacent edges. Typhoon cables, strapped to limestone boulders that abound on the site, braced supporting aluminum masts. Access to the site, Morgan stipulated, might be by means of a helicopter, or an inflated rubber raft through the mid-Pacific surf, or by some other method.

The Guam Vacation House design demonstrated several concepts that would resurface in Morgan's subsequent work. These include portability of buildings and components, the use of such twentieth-century materials as weatherproof plastic fabric and lightweight/high-strength metals, mass production of components for distant sites, and interchangeability of components to alter the size or shapes of buildings. The design was well adapted to the climate of the Marianas, with removable panels to enhance cross-ventilation and waterproof sheeting capable of withstanding tropical rainstorms. It also was radically different from other student submissions, which generally followed the model of a typical suburban house. Morgan passed his first assignment.

During the early 1950s two widely divergent directions in design education greeted students at the GSD. When William Morgan returned to Harvard to pursue his professional degree in architecture, he found a new design curriculum in place. Josep Lluís Sert was the new dean at GSD, having replaced Joseph Hudnut in 1953, and his experience in Latin American architecture and urbanism was increasingly imprinted on the school's philosophy. In addition to implementing its new design direction, the GSD restored architectural history courses that had been deemphasized during Walter Gropius's tenure as chair, which ended in 1952.[8]

Figure 11. Sketch of Morgan's design for a Guam Vacation House, an early assignment for graduate architecture students at GSD. Morgan sought to blend traditional themes of Guam architecture with lightweight, advanced materials that could be transported by air to remote spots. Courtesy of the William Morgan Collection, University of Florida Libraries.

Figure 12. Drawing of Morgan's design for a Guam Vacation House. Courtesy of the William Morgan Collection, University of Florida Libraries.

Left: Figure 13. Morgan (*left*) presenting to a GSD jury. From the Morgan family.

Above: Figure 14. Morgan (*left*) with fellow students Michael Zimmer (*center*) and Nelson Chin. From the Morgan family.

While working with Paul Rudolph, Morgan had long hours of discussions with important figures like Philip Johnson and Serge Chermayeff, which inspired him to question the GSD's new curriculum. Emboldened by his experiences in Rudolph's office, he voiced his strong objections to a design problem introduced in class, which Morgan described as yet another plaza surrounded by low-rise concrete buildings. During discussion about the assignment, Morgan postulated that the problem would be well suited to Cuba, or perhaps Colombia, but he thought it had little relevance in Boston or even Jacksonville. "What happened to steel frame high-rise buildings, the standards for designs in the United States?" he asked. Morgan's outburst unsettled the class and stirred debate. As Morgan recalled, Dean Sert ultimately approved of his suggestions and modified the assignment, but Morgan still found most of his fellow students' final design presentations to be disappointing and unsophisticated, at best.

With the birth of his son, Newton, in November 1956, pressure on Morgan to provide for his family increased. Under Dean Sert, the GSD offered a three-year degree that enabled students to earn a bachelor's in architecture, rather than a master's degree. Morgan and other students considered this program, nicknamed the "shortcut," to be a method for weeding out less promising students and making space for new candidates.

Morgan's lack of income and increased responsibilities made for a seemingly impossible situation and forced him to consider the shortcut and to leave Harvard early, but with a lesser degree that still would allow him to work as an architect. "I was going to take the shortcut to get this degree so I could go out there and start training in an architect's office," Morgan said. "I had filled that out and sent in what was, effectively, my resignation from the school full-time. I was simply going broke. I was going so broke, it wouldn't take much to drop off the cliff."

Shortly after Morgan submitted the resignation papers, Huson Jackson, one of the GSD faculty members and a partner of the firm that came to be known as Sert, Jackson and Gourley, contacted Morgan and told him he had made a mistake and had checked the wrong box on his form. Morgan believed Jackson wanted to see him leave GSD, and it was to his great surprise that he learned the opposite. Jackson respected Morgan for his work in Paul Rudolph's office and presented Morgan with an offer to become what was, in effect, a junior faculty member. "I had only an A.B. degree," Morgan recalled, "but I had worked for Rudolph. That was the equivalent of a degree in itself!"

The major responsibility of the "junior faculty" position was to design a lecture series. The GSD earmarked funds for the program, and Morgan contacted architects, invited them to speak, and oversaw their arrangements. Richard Neutra, whom Morgan had met on Guam, was among the speakers he brought to the GSD. "I would meet people like Neutra at Logan

Airport, collect their luggage, and take them wherever I had made arrangements for them to stay," Morgan recounted. "Then I would take them to the lecture hall, make introductory remarks, arrange cocktail parties, and provide whatever they needed."

Morgan considered his lecture series "excellent," and the lecturers "world-class." They welcomed the chance to appear at Harvard and participate in the series. For Morgan, the lecture series and his previous experience in Rudolph's office were important steps in his career: "In the end, I got to know a lot of very important people very early in my professional career. I knew the top people in American design, and I was associated with that group of people. I don't know where it comes in the becoming of an architect, but at some point it is very helpful to have a good standing in the community—the architectural community—and to have a reputation that one can rely on."

Morgan described the GSD faculty as "unbelievable," and he greatly admired Walter Gropius, the founder of Weimar's Bauhaus school. After Hitler came to power in 1933 and closed the Bauhaus, GSD's dean Joseph Hudnut invited Gropius to join Harvard as a professor and chair of Harvard's Department of Architecture. Gropius remained chair from 1937 until 1952, when he stepped down during a dispute over the curriculum and faculty.[9] But Gropius remained a presence at GSD even after his resignation, and he played a role in selecting Hudnut's successor, Josep Lluís Sert, who continued to move the faculty and curriculum toward modernism.[10]

Gropius held a bias against architectural history because he thought each building should be created anew, without influences of history or research. He had abolished history courses at the Bauhaus and wished to do the same at GSD.[11] Morgan himself believed the "paucity of architectural history" was "the foremost weakness of the Gropius curriculum." Although architectural history was deemphasized under Gropius and had only recently been restored when Morgan attended the GSD, the understanding of architectural history became central to Morgan. He benefited from a close relationship with Vienna-born Eduard Sekler, whose lectures solidified Morgan's reverence for earlier architects and builders. Many years later, Sekler would author the foreword to both the Spreiregen and McCarter books about Morgan's body of work. Morgan described Sekler's influence on his development as an architect:

> Sekler was an architect, but was also a particularly distinguished historian. I have never seen the equivalent of his knowledge of architectural history. Every year at the GSD, one quarter of the curriculum was devoted to history; one quarter was devoted to structural, mechanical, electrical, plumbing, and that engineering kind of stuff; and one half of the time was devoted to design. Typically, if the student passed design, it really didn't matter if you passed the other two. However, I was extremely interested in what Dr. Sekler had to say, and he appreciated my interests as well.
>
> I found, not from working for Rudolph but more so from Sekler, that knowledge from history is part and parcel of the making of an architect. If you don't know where you've been, you won't know where you're going. When I was in the navy, you looked at your wake to see what course the ship was making. Same thing.

Sekler's courses ranged across the world and the span of time in a comprehensive and incisive sweep that examined complex civilizations and the cities they built. Morgan's first course covered Egypt, Nubia, the Lower Nile Valley, and classical Greece. The second began in Rome, covered the Middle Ages, and then continued onward. "In all of these classes I was very impressed with Dr. Sekler," Morgan noted. "He had had a way of getting to the beginning of things. That was one of the strong influences on me. What the beginnings were, where it started. His message was: 'Don't worry too much about where we are, worry about where we have been. An idea will come from some point of beginning. If it doesn't have that richness, if it doesn't have those roots, it really isn't too worth your time.' That was Sekler all over."

Morgan distinguished himself at the GSD. The school encouraged students to come up with ideas, to express them, and to defend them. In the process they were required to describe clearly the concept, the context, and the use of material for a project. Morgan's work in

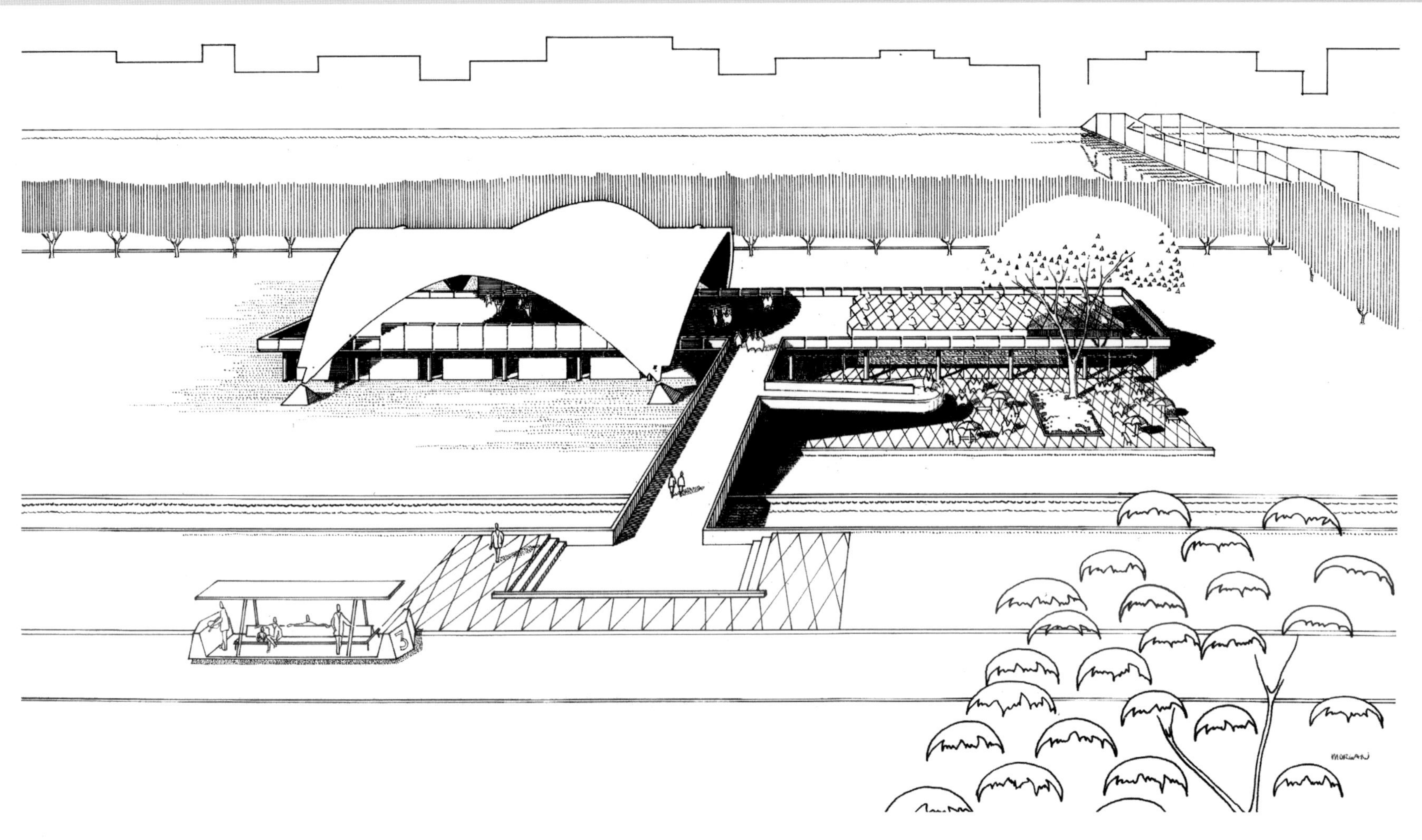

Figure 15. Drawing of Morgan's design satisfying a 1957 GSD assignment to design a community center for a small city in western Massachusetts. At this early stage Morgan evidently shared Paul Rudolph's interest in expressive roof designs. GSD History Collection: Student Affairs. Courtesy of the Frances Loeb Library, Harvard University Graduate School of Design.

Figure 16. Part of a submission for a four-student project concerning an elementary school in Concord, Massachusetts. The design prominently included a corrugated plywood roof. GSD History Collection: Student Affairs. Courtesy of the Frances Loeb Library, Harvard University Graduate School of Design.

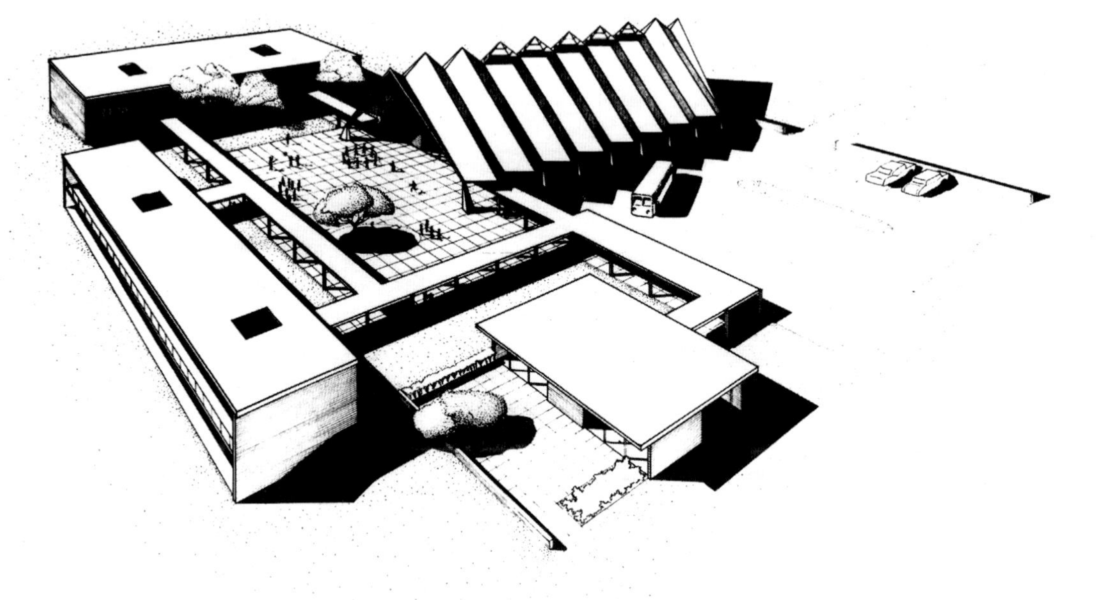

CONCORD ELEMENTARY SCHOOL

An economical eighteen classroom elementary school and kindergarten was proposed for a rolling site near Concord, Massachusetts. A team of four students designed the school shown here, prepared preliminary working drawings, compiled a brochure, and made initial cost estimates. Class-room wings are of lift slab construction and are accessible on two levels from split level entries, eliminating corridors and providing through ventillation and optimum lighting conditions for each classroom. A corrugated plywood honeycomb roof economically spans the multipurpose building. (Part of a six week team problem with criticism, December 1956)

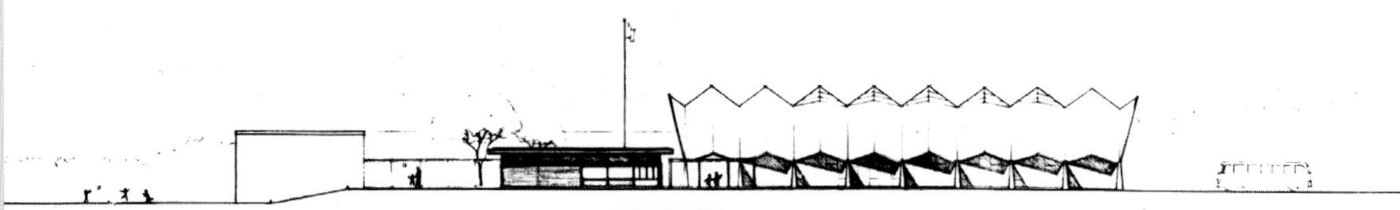

William Morgan
arch 2-3 1956-57

graduate school foreshadowed many of the themes that came into play and evolved through his professional practice: earth architecture, experimentation, awareness of architecture's historical roots, and a strong interplay of buildings with their surroundings.

First Experiment with Earth Architecture

The design for a Cowboy Hall of Fame was a 1957 national competition, and the GSD made this an assignment for its architecture students. The museum site lay in the wide-open space of Oklahoma, which reminded Morgan of similar landscapes in the vicinity of Las Vegas, Nevada, where he had spent three summers in the early 1940s. Morgan recalled:

> The site consists of a broad, unspoiled plain bounded by a distinctive line of hills in the limitless expanse of the Southwest. From a design point of view, placing a conventional museum building on the site—no matter where—seemed inappropriate both to the site and to the spirit of the memorial. After weeks of failed attempts to design a building on the site, I realized that the appropriate memorial was the site itself.[12]

Morgan had no interest in designing a conventional museum, and the result was the future architect's first experience at incorporating earth architecture into his designs. In Morgan's vision, the site would be integral to a building that would honor the spirit of the art, culture, and history of the American West.

Morgan proposed sculpting a ridge along the site's edge. An elevated causeway would invite visitors to leave their cars in the parking area and follow a processional to a grand plaza carved into an earthen ridge. Here huge murals and an exhibition hall in the shape of a truncated pyramid would house the museum's exhibits. This design was Morgan's first experience in sculpting earth, a theme that became more important through his career.

Recalled Morgan: "The proposal shocked my professors, but the possibility was intriguing. I began to look more carefully at Frank Lloyd Wright's inquiries into earth architecture, for

SALOON

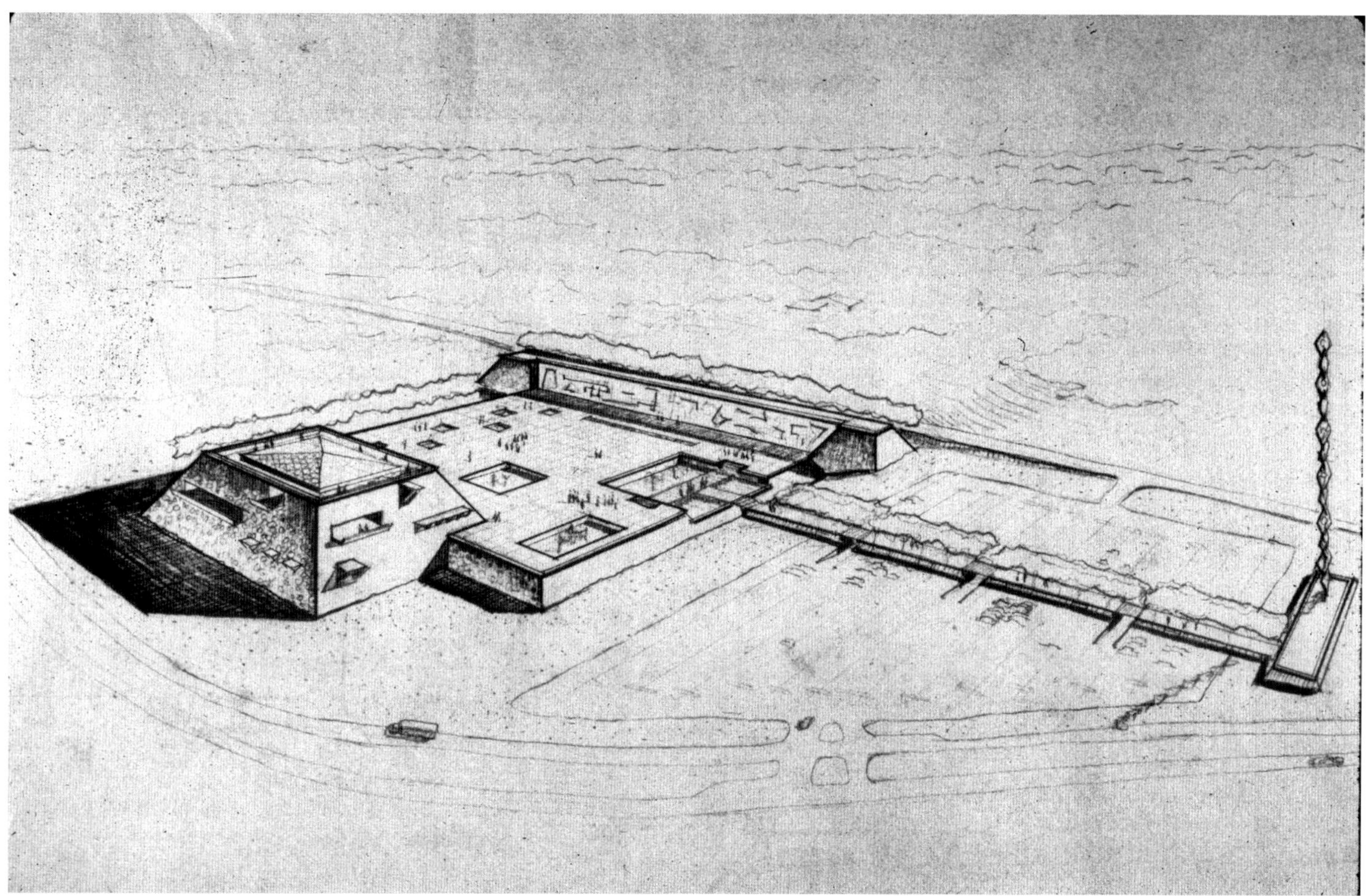

Facing page: Figure 17. Drawing of Morgan's submission for a 1957 design competition for the National Cowboy Hall of Fame and Western Heritage Museum in Oklahoma. Courtesy of the William Morgan Collection, University of Florida Libraries.

Above: Figure 18. Drawing of submission for a 1957 design competition for the National Cowboy Hall of Fame and Western Heritage Museum in Oklahoma. This was Morgan's first use of earth architecture. Courtesy of the William Morgan Collection, University of Florida Libraries.

example, his proposed Detroit Auto Workers' Housing and second Jacobs House."[13] Morgan remained proud of his effort, which he regarded as a dynamic expression in a monumental, timeless setting. As with the Guam Vacation House, this project touched on themes that Morgan would explore more thoroughly throughout his professional career.

Later during his years at GSD Morgan joined a four-student team as part of a worldwide open design competition for Toronto's new city hall. Morgan designed the roof for the complex with four enormous "trees," the branches of which cantilevered out like limbs from the tree trunks supporting an undulating fiberglass roof with skylights that admitted daylight as though filtered through a canopy of leaves. Later in his career Morgan worked with refined versions of these early "trees" in his design for the Police Memorial Building in Jacksonville and in Fort Lauderdale's Federal Building and Courthouse.

The 1958 competition attracted more than five hundred entrants from around the world, from which eight finalist teams were selected. One of those teams included Morgan and his classmates John Andrews, Macy DuBois, and W. Byron Ireland. (Andrews would later design Gund Hall, home of the GSD since 1972.) The design was submitted under Andrews's name because he was the only team member who was a graduate architect.[14] A group of faculty from the GSD also made a submission to the competition, but—according to Morgan—their submission failed to make even the initial cut. Finnish architect Viljo Revell won the competition.

Following his graduation from Harvard's Graduate School of Design in 1958, and with strong recommendations from the Harvard faculty, Morgan won a Fulbright grant, which enabled the newly minted architect to study in Rome for a year. He, Bunny, and their two-year-old son, Newton, boarded a ship for Italy in 1958. That experience deepened Morgan's perspective on architectural history, contributed to his understanding of other elements of design, and piqued his interest in pursuing research themes later in his career.

Above: Figure 19. Morgan was part of a student team that submitted a well-regarded entry to the 1956–57 Toronto City Hall design competition. Courtesy of the William Morgan Collection, University of Florida Libraries.

Right: Figure 20. GSD students with model of Toronto City Hall submission. *Left to right*: William Morgan, Carl Luckenbach, and Byron Ireland. From the Morgan family.

Above: Figure 21. Passport photo for young Newton Morgan taken prior to the family's travel to Italy with Morgan's Fulbright grant, 1958. From the Morgan family.

Right: Figure 22. William and Bunny Morgan in Venice, while studying under a Fulbright grant. From the Morgan family.

In Rome Morgan worked with renowned Italian structural engineer Pier Luigi Nervi studying spanning systems. Under the direction of Nervi's assistant, Sergio Musmeci, Morgan designed a spectacular tensile roof canopy for an outdoor theater that seated hundreds of spectators in an earthen bowl. Although Morgan described the structure as "unrealistic," the magazine *L'Architettura* printed a feature in both Italian and English on his proposal.

5

A Career Begins

Morgan's work for Paul Rudolph, his master's degree from GSD, and his Fulbright in Rome provided him with valuable experience, but to practice architecture in the United States one needs a professional degree, a passing grade on a state board licensing examination, and a formal residency working in the office of a registered architect. While in Rome Morgan received a letter from Ivan Smith, offering him a position with the important Jacksonville firm Reynolds, Smith and Hills (RS&H) upon his return to the United States. Morgan happily accepted the job, and he returned to Jacksonville after the Fulbright ended and went to work for the company. But Morgan quickly learned that what RS&H wanted from him was not the kind of forward-thinking architecture he wanted to create.

"I joined the firm but soon found that instead of being concerned with great beauty and really great architecture, they were more of an engineering company," Morgan said. "That was not to my taste, and I did not fare very well there. I did attempt at first to design something . . . and it went over like a lead balloon."

Morgan remained at RS&H just long enough to meet his residency requirements and pass the state exam. Then he resigned with a flourish. "With all that done, I just walked out the door at Reynolds, Smith and Hills," Morgan recalled. "I said, 'Goodbye boys,' but nobody noticed that I had left."

He was now a full-fledged architect eager to make his mark. "I was free to get out on my own, which I did immediately, but I had just no prospects," he said. "Not a single job. And nobody would know me from Adam's house cat."

Now practicing on his own and with no clients, the first order of business for Morgan was to establish an office for his fledgling practice and a home for his young family. Morgan had little in the way of savings and an uncertain cash flow, other than Bunny's salary from teaching art in the public schools of Duval County, Florida. Given the Morgans' tight finances, they needed a structure that was economical both to build and to inhabit. Morgan's solution was to build a single structure in 1961 that would incorporate an apartment for the family, a small office, and two one-bedroom apartments for rental income. He designed and largely built the structure himself using common and inexpensive materials, such as plywood and concrete block.

Although the family budget dictated economical materials and pragmatic purpose, Morgan unleashed his creativity and design sensibility in formulating the project. He looked to the grand eighth-century Basilica of Sant'Ambrogio in Milan for his inspiration, a church he had visited while in Italy on the Fulbright. The structure consists of vaulted bays, each two stories high, that open to one another and create a grand interior space that draws the eye and the spirit upward.

For 1611 Ocean Boulevard, Morgan built a simple one-story structure based on twelve 16-foot-square modules that opened into one another to create large interior spaces that could be closed off to form smaller spaces. He created triangular roof panels out of thirty-three folded-plywood plates. The plates formed an eight-foot overhang across the front of the building, with the points of the triangles forming a zigzag pattern down the length of the building. Clerestory windows allowed diffused natural light into the interior and gave a glimpse of the adjoining ceiling vaults repeating through the structure beyond the room one occupies, just like the vaults at Sant'Ambrogio.

Above: Figure 23. 1611 Ocean Boulevard, Atlantic Beach, Florida. Morgan's own practice began with this building, which originally included three apartments, one of which was inhabited by his family of four, and an office. From the Morgan family.

Right: Figure 24. Interior of 1611 Ocean Boulevard, highlighting the vaulted plywood ceiling and clerestory windows. Courtesy of the William Morgan Collection, University of Florida Libraries. Photo by Alexandre Georges.

Figure 25. Contemporary (2015) photo of 1611 Ocean Boulevard, recently restored. Photo by the author.

Despite intense development in Atlantic Beach since 1961, the structure remains much as it was designed, although the architectural office has since been converted into another apartment.

The fresh and well-executed design at 1611 Ocean Boulevard paid off for the fledgling architect and became the departure point for a reputation for bold design that accompanied his career for more than a half century.

One day, as Morgan worked on 1611 Ocean Boulevard, a neighbor approached. Al James had watched Morgan's building take shape, and he liked what he saw. He told the architect he owned the empty lot across the street and asked him to design a home there for his young family. After Morgan's mundane assignments with RS&H, here was an opportunity to focus on creative design concepts for a client. His investment in 1611 Ocean Boulevard served an additional purpose by showing—in concrete block, glass, and plywood—just the kind of architectural energy that Morgan planned to bring to his practice.

For the James family Morgan designed a small, inexpensive, and decidedly modern house that accommodated a family of five. The house included a dramatic two-story living room with fireplace, a feature that reappeared in Morgan's later low-cost projects. Thus Al James became Morgan's first client and provided his first architectural commission.

When the James Residence was completed, Morgan sent several 35mm slides, plans, and sections to the journal *Architectural Record*, just as he had seen Rudolph do with his projects. It paid off. The magazine sent photographer Alexandre Georges down to photograph the house, and it was subsequently published as the first of eight Morgan projects to appear in that highly regarded periodical. Georges also became a close friend and advised Morgan on publishing and promoting his work. The James Residence appeared in *Architectural Record* in May 1963 and in *Florida Architect* in June 1963.

Although his work had been featured in architectural journals, Morgan still struggled. He took on a variety of small commercial projects that demonstrated the architect's preference for creative solutions, even for mundane purposes.

Facing page: Figure 26. View from northeast, former Maryland Fried Chicken building, now home to Embassy Barber Shop, Neptune Beach, Florida. Early in his architectural career, Morgan stayed in business with a series of modest commissions. Photo by Brad Chesivoir.

Shortly after the 1961 completion of the James Residence, Morgan's former employer RS&H was approached to design a canopy to shelter the gasoline pumps at a filling station in the small town of Palatka, Florida, south of Jacksonville on the St. Johns River. As the job was too small for such a large firm, RS&H was charitable enough to pass it to Morgan and his young practice. Thanks to Morgan's creativity, the Clyde M. Rozier Sinclair service station subsequently included a hyperbolic paraboloid canopy made out of cast-in-place concrete. This element floated above the gasoline pumps like a large concrete umbrella. Morgan regarded it as a spectacular structure for such a rural community.

A high school friend turned developer also helped Morgan establish his practice. Early in 1961 Stanley Teate asked Morgan to design a small fried chicken restaurant in Neptune Beach, Florida. The Maryland Fried Chicken building was a modest rectangular box with a cantilevered roof to provide shade and shelter. Where the cantilever emerged from the building, two lighted boxes featured signs reading: "Eat In" and "Take Out." This simple, practical, modernist structure functions today as the Embassy Barber Shop on Penman Road.

Later that year, a prominent builder, the S. S. Jacobs Company, hired Morgan to design offices for Brundage Motors, a parts distributor for Volkswagen in Florida, Georgia, and South Carolina. The building was inexpensively built—at about four dollars per square foot—with 90-foot sides composed of six 15-foot, cast-in-place, tilt-up panels. The architect had no great fondness for the building, but at 16,200 square feet, it was then his largest completed design. The Brundage Motors facility is now part of a complex owned by Vulcan Materials Company. The project was also Morgan's first association with Preston Haskell, who had recently been hired by Jacobs and served as construction superintendent on this assignment.

Three years after designing the chicken restaurant, Morgan completed a second commission for Stanley Teate. Morgan was glad for the work, but it was not very profitable, he confided. "The fee wasn't enough to feed the dog," Morgan confessed, and the family continued to rely on Bunny's salary.

110
Embassy Barber Shop
Hours Of Operation
Saturday
Sunday Closed
Cash & Checks Only
Embassy
Barber Shop

Teate wanted a small commercial building on the frontage road of Arlington Expressway in Jacksonville's Arlington neighborhood. For Morgan, the job afforded an opportunity to experiment with roof design.

In the E.L.K. Oil Company Building, completed in 1964, Morgan invented an efficient solution to the cost of roof vaults. In vaulting a concrete structure, one typically must build a form, cast the concrete on it, and then remove the formwork. The difficulty and expense of this process limits its use in contemporary architecture. Morgan came up with an efficient solution. "Why not let gravity be the shaper?" he remembered thinking. "If we put up two parallel steel beams, then we can take our open-weave steel reinforcing mesh and drape it from one beam to the next, and it will become both the formwork and the roof." Morgan erected parallel steel beams at the roof level of the bays. He draped steel-mesh rebar between the beams, forming curves between the beams that resembled inverted barrel vaults. Next, he laid planks of rigid insulation on the mesh and sprayed Gunite concrete, a material more typically used for swimming pool construction—and one he would later use in other innovative contexts—on the top and bottom of each vault. The result is a series of vaults cantilevered out above glazed entry walls. The finished rectangular building consists of identical bays with swooping rooflines and column-free interiors. Economical to erect and maintain, the vaulted structure continues in use today, more than fifty years after its original construction.

The E.L.K. Oil Company Building, with its catenary roofline, echoes an earlier and better-known building by Morgan's mentor, Paul Rudolph. The Healy Cocoon House in Sarasota featured a roof constructed with drooping cables, covered with hardware cloth and then sprayed with a flexible vinyl plastic called "Cocoon."[1] Rudolph's innovative building was plagued by the leaky Cocoon material.[2] According to its current owners, the real estate and development firm Meadows, Inc., the E.L.K. Oil Company Building is leak-proof. The company converted the building to its present configuration with ten individual office units.

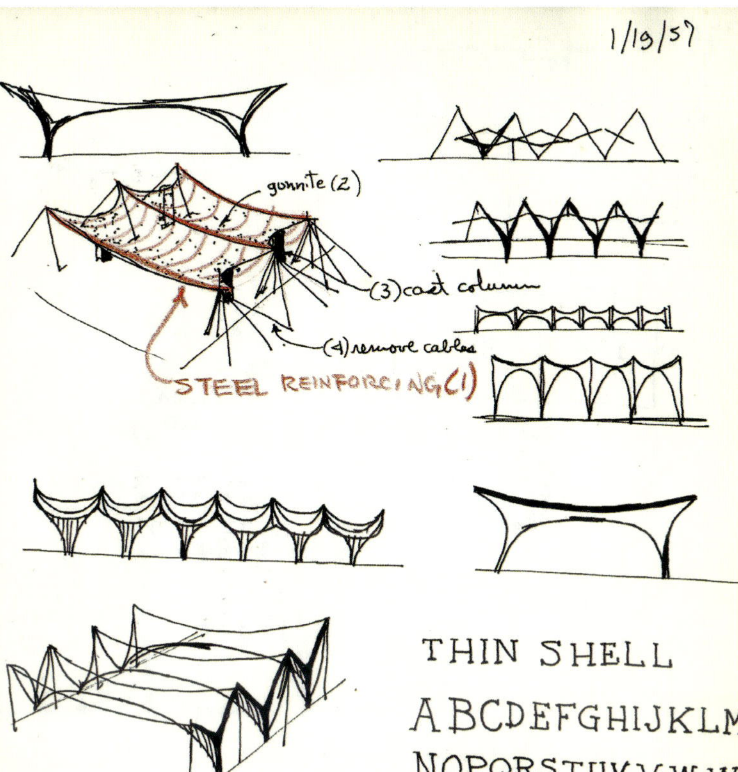

Far left: Figure 27. Sketches by William Morgan while at GSD that foreshadowed the E.L.K. Oil Company design, which was completed seven years later. Courtesy of the William Morgan Collection, University of Florida Libraries.

Left: Figure 28. Construction of the E.L.K. Oil Company Building, Jacksonville, Florida, circa 1964. The photo highlights the method of fabricating the building's catenary roof. Courtesy of the William Morgan Collection, University of Florida Libraries.

Figure 29. E.L.K. Oil Company Building, Jacksonville, Florida. Roof sections prepared for application of Gunite concrete. Courtesy of the William Morgan Collection, University of Florida Libraries.

Figure 30. Contemporary (2015) photo of E.L.K. Oil Company Building, highlighting its catenary roof constructed with Gunite concrete. The building is now owned and partially occupied by Meadows Incorporated. Photo by Brad Chesivoir.

Figure 31. Novelty postcard from Peru with image of William Morgan at center, from his Wheelwright Prize travels in 1964. From the Morgan family.

Wheelwright Prize

Banking on his prominently publicized early successes, Morgan applied for and won the GSD's Arthur W. Wheelwright Traveling Fellowship in 1964. The Wheelwright is a financial grant awarded to "talented early-career architects worldwide."[3] The prize, which has been awarded since 1935, currently provides fellowship recipients with $100,000 for research and travel. Past recipients have included Paul Rudolph, Eliot Noyes, William Wurster, Christopher Tunnard, I. M. Pei, John Haro, Klaus Herdeg, Farès el-Dahdah, Adele Santos, and Linda Pollak.[4] Receiving the prize enabled Morgan to spend a year touring the world to study architectural and archaeological sites, including many related to earth architecture.

By the time he applied for the fellowship, Morgan had accumulated an excellent collection of black-and-white photographs that Alexandre Georges had shot of his work. Morgan included the photos in his application: "The photos themselves were beautiful. Add to that the fact that they had been published in the top journals," Morgan commented. "To have some jerk student do an end run like that made a lot of teeth chatter. A faculty member who was on the selection committee was Eduard Sekler, my great friend and teacher. I believe he was one of the reasons I was fortunate enough to receive the award."

Although his practice demonstrated increasing vitality, Morgan and Bunny traveled the world over the next two years, while juggling the responsibilities of work and family. "With the Wheelwright you could go anywhere you wanted; you didn't report to anyone," Morgan recalled. "One slice would finance our travel in the Western Hemisphere and the other in the Eastern Hemisphere." The Morgans minimized separation from the architectural practice and family by dividing the Wheelwright explorations into separate one-month journeys. It helped that his mother was living in one of the two rental units at 1611 Ocean Boulevard, and she could conveniently watch the couple's two young sons. A draftsman watched the business.

With the Wheelwright money Morgan first traveled in Latin America and the Caribbean, visiting pre-Columbian sites in Honduras, Guatemala, Mexico, and Peru—where he visited Machu Picchu.

The eastern phase of Morgan's Wheelwright explorations started in Japan with Ise and other important Shinto shrines that he had wanted to visit during his navy service. From there he went to Cambodia and Bangkok. He then proceeded west to India, with visits to Delhi and Chandigarh, where buildings by Le Corbusier had recently been completed or were nearing completion. Morgan later went to Iran and various sites linked to battles of Darius the Great. After departing Iran, he visited Petra in Jordan and then made his way to Egypt and down the Nile Valley to Abu Simbel and the temples built by Pharaoh Ramses II, which were relocated from the site of the Aswan High Dam.

Among other things, the Wheelwright Prize enabled Morgan to begin serious research into a type of architecture referred to as earth architecture, which uses earth to build various kinds of human environments. Morgan recognized that modern techniques of molding and shaping the earth had become advanced but were also overlooked by architects and city planners. "I began to realize what can be done by shaping the earth to reinforce architecture and create dignified settings for serious works," he said. As part of his research, Morgan took core samples from thirteen examples of earth architecture around the world, including from Teotihuacán (Mexico), Acoma Pueblo (United States), Baphuon (Cambodia), and Petra (Jordan).

Morgan's research under the auspices of the Wheelwright Prize led to an unpublished volume on earth architecture containing sixty-nine pages of the architect/author's own drawings. Some of the content—although none of the drawings—ultimately found its way into his four books on ancient architecture as well as his 2008 work on the subject, *Earth Architecture: From Ancient to Modern*, published by the University Press of Florida. Both the unpublished work and the 2008 book rely on a large reservoir of research materials provided by Ludwig Glaeser, a curator with the Museum of Modern Art in New York. "Ludwig sent us a crate as big as a casket with information on buildings made out of earth from all over the world. It

Figure 32. Sample page from an unpublished draft of a book on earth architecture by William Morgan. Unlike *Earth Architecture: From Ancient to Modern*, published in 2008, this work was entirely illustrated with Morgan's own drawings. From the Morgan family.

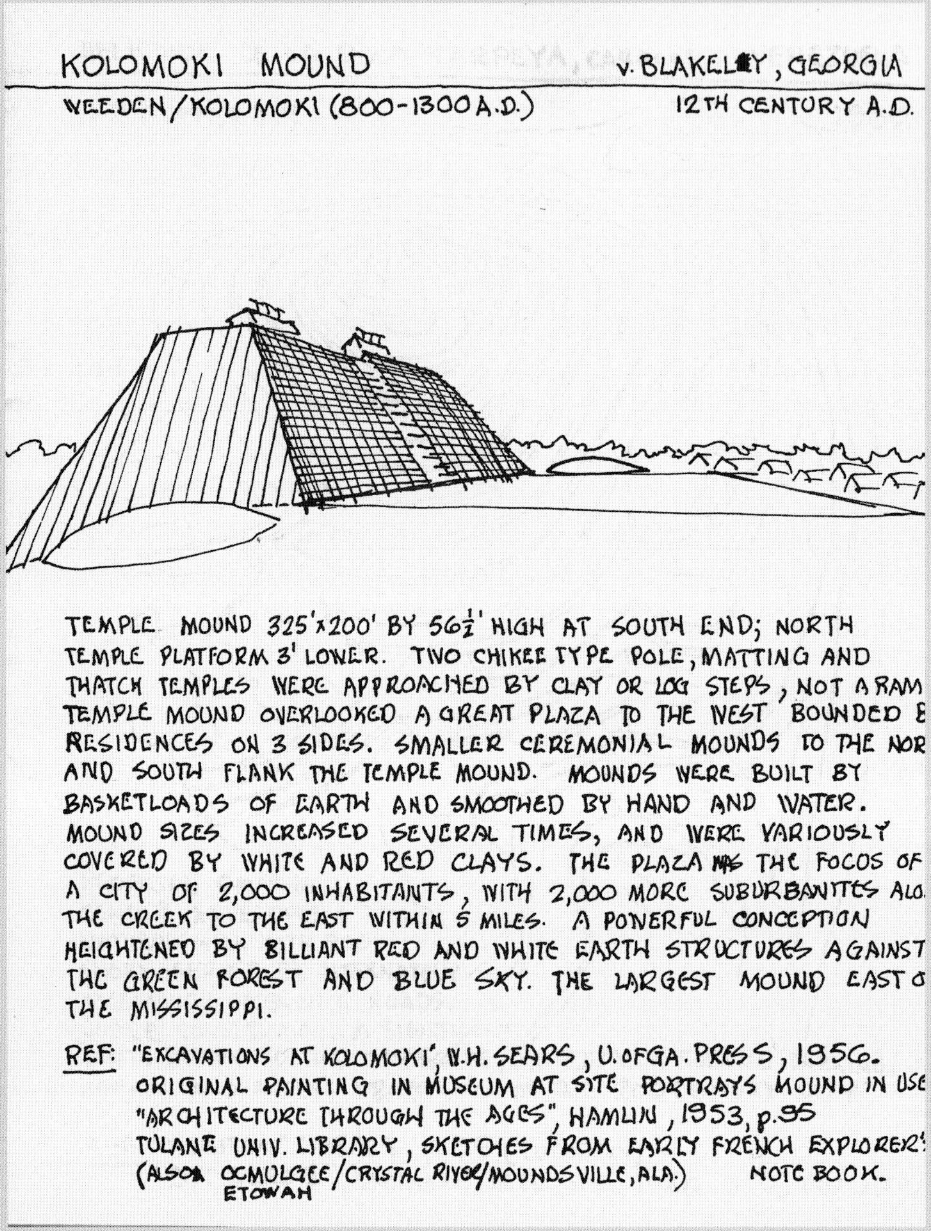

KOLOMOKI MOUND v. BLAKELEY, GEORGIA

WEEDEN/KOLOMOKI (800-1300 A.D.) 12TH CENTURY A.D.

TEMPLE MOUND 325'x200' BY 56½' HIGH AT SOUTH END; NORTH TEMPLE PLATFORM 3' LOWER. TWO CHIKEE TYPE POLE, MATTING AND THATCH TEMPLES WERE APPROACHED BY CLAY OR LOG STEPS, NOT A RAM TEMPLE MOUND OVERLOOKED A GREAT PLAZA TO THE WEST BOUNDED B RESIDENCES ON 3 SIDES. SMALLER CEREMONIAL MOUNDS TO THE NOR AND SOUTH FLANK THE TEMPLE MOUND. MOUNDS WERE BUILT BY BASKETLOADS OF EARTH AND SMOOTHED BY HAND AND WATER. MOUND SIZES INCREASED SEVERAL TIMES, AND WERE VARIOUSLY COVERED BY WHITE AND RED CLAYS. THE PLAZA WAS THE FOCOS OF A CITY OF 2,000 INHABITANTS, WITH 2,000 MORE SUBURBANITES ALO THE CREEK TO THE EAST WITHIN 5 MILES. A POWERFUL CONCEPTION HEIGHTENED BY BILLIANT RED AND WHITE EARTH STRUCTURES AGAINST THE GREEN FOREST AND BLUE SKY. THE LARGEST MOUND EAST O THE MISSISSIPPI.

REF: "EXCAVATIONS AT KOLOMOKI", W.H. SEARS, U. OF GA. PRESS, 1956.
ORIGINAL PAINTING IN MUSEUM AT SITE PORTRAYS MOUND IN USE
"ARCHITECTURE THROUGH THE AGES", HAMLIN, 1953, p. 95
TULANE UNIV. LIBRARY, SKETCHES FROM EARLY FRENCH EXPLORER'S NOTE BOOK.
(ALSO OCMULGEE/CRYSTAL RIVER/MOUNDSVILLE, ALA.)
ETOWAH

was so big that Ludwig asked, 'Why don't you take this first segment of the Eastern U.S. and write about that?'" remembered Morgan's wife, Bunny.

Flying over the Okefenokee Swamp years after he returned from his Wheelwright travels, Morgan remembered a related experience flying over the vast, inundated lowlands between Siem Reap and Angkor Wat in northern Cambodia. From the air, the Okefenokee Swamp and the swamp of Angkor struck him as interchangeable, but a critical difference had impressed itself on Morgan's imagination. "The difference was the highly civilized buildings of the Khmer compared to the less advanced construction from early inhabitants of the southeastern United States," Morgan said. "There [in Cambodia], I caught glimpses of history: the ruins of Angkor Wat, Angkor Thom, the Baphuon, and many other related monuments. The ancient Khmer builders created geometrically precise platforms of earth surrounded by moats and a number of reflecting ponds and lakes interconnected by shaded pedestrian walkways," Morgan said.

Back in Jacksonville, ship builder David Rawls asked Morgan to design a new house for him on Pottsburg Creek in 1963. The house was completed in 1965. Along with his brother, Rawls owned a business and had constructed merchant vessels in Jacksonville during World War II. When he approached Morgan, Rawls was serving as executive director of the Jacksonville Port Authority.[5] "He was thoroughly conversant with steel construction and thus had an appreciation for residential designs primarily built of steel and glass," Morgan said.

For Rawls, Morgan designed a rectangular two-story house that was anything but ordinary. Steel beams concealed in the roof cantilever above the bedrooms, which in turn hover over carports on the ground level. The two second-floor bedrooms extend to the end of the building's cantilevered walls. Stone towers on either end of the residence contain mechanical systems and bathrooms. One enters the residence under a seven-and-a-half-foot-high balcony into a two-story living room.

After the Rawls site had been cleared for construction, Morgan instructed the contractor to stake out the first-floor plan in order to ensure that the foundation would be located

Above: Figure 33. East side of the Rawls Residence, Jacksonville, Florida, with open views of the pool area and tidal creek. Courtesy of the William Morgan Collection, University of Florida Libraries. Photo by Alexandre Georges.

Facing page, left: Figure 34. Circular stairway off cantilevered second floor of Rawls Residence. The building's clients desired direct access to the swimming pool for every room. The stairs were later removed. Courtesy of the William Morgan Collection, University of Florida Libraries. Photo by Alexandre Georges.

Facing page, right: Figure 35. Early sketch for Rawls Residence. The final design included a cantilevered second floor extending twelve feet on either side. Courtesy of the William Morgan Collection, University of Florida Libraries.

7@12=84'
CARPT. 20'x24'
LIVING 20'x24'
20'
CLOS.
CLOS.
12x17
BR
12x13
BR

Facing page: Figure 36. Contemporary view (2015) from the east of Rawls Residence. Photo by Brad Chesivoir.

Left: Figure 37. Contemporary interior view of Rawls Residence looking east. Among other changes, the original terrazzo floors have been replaced with ceramic tile. The two-story living room remains. Photo by Brad Chesivoir.

correctly. David Rawls happened to be on the site that day, and he asked Morgan what the stakes and strings represented. After the architect explained their significance, the client grew apprehensive. He thought the rooms would be too small. To allay the client's fears, Morgan increased the width of the layout by two feet on both floors, and the construction cost was adjusted accordingly. But when walls and ceilings were completed, Rawls was surprised by the excessively large rooms. From this experience, Morgan learned an appreciation for a layman's difficulty in comprehending volumes from two-dimensional plans.

Above: Figure 38. The Williamson Residence in Ponte Vedra Beach, Florida, continued to explore the interplay between vertical masses and cantilevered horizontal structures. From the Morgan family.

Right: Figure 39. Drawing of Williamson Residence, Ponte Vedra Beach, Florida. As with the Rawls Residence, this was a rectilinear design formed around prominent masonry piers. Courtesy of the William Morgan Collection, University of Florida Libraries.

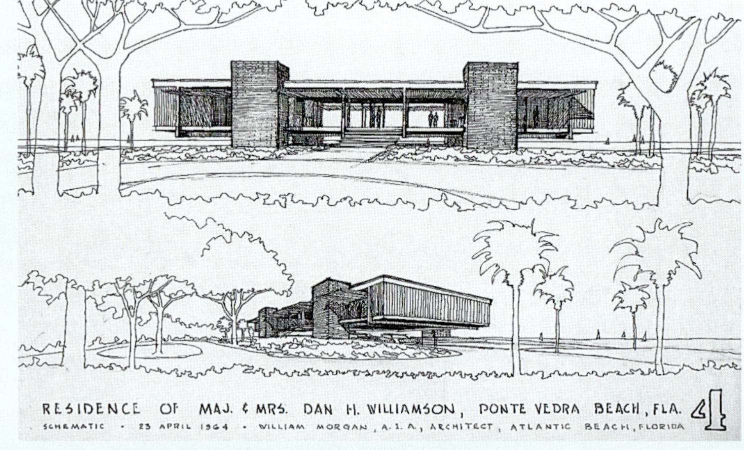

Figure 40. In 2016 Hurricane Matthew severely damaged the Williamson Residence. Photo by the author.

As the Rawls project neared completion, Morgan sent 35mm slides of its design and construction to Barclay F. Gordon, an associate editor of *Architectural Record* magazine. Gordon was impressed and dispatched Alexandre Georges to photograph the project for an upcoming issue. According to Morgan, Gordon taped one of the slides to his window facing 43rd Street in Manhattan and invited everybody who came into his office to put a dollar into a kitty and guess the cost of this project. As Morgan recalled, the estimates ranged from $450,000 up to well over $1 million. In fact, the house cost only around $45,000 because of its economical design and construction—always a point of pride for Morgan. The Rawls Residence was featured in *Architectural Record*'s May 1965 issue and was one of twenty residences that received

Facing page: Figure 41. Goodloe Residence, Ponte Vedra Beach, Florida. View looking west from the beach showing interplay of prefabricated rectangular boxes. Open ground floor offered some protection from flooding. Courtesy of the William Morgan Collection, University of Florida Libraries.

the publication's award of excellence that year.[6] It was also featured in *Arts & Architecture*, the *New York Times*, *Bauen + Wohnen*, *Florida Architect*, and *L'Architecture d'Aujourd'hui.*

Shortly after Morgan designed the Rawls Residence, the Williamson family commissioned him to design a home to sit on a then remote oceanfront site in Ponte Vedra Beach, Florida. Morgan's vision included a two-story building, with its primary spaces on the upper level and a garage and utility spaces on the lower level recessed into the sand dunes. This arrangement provided commanding views and favorable breezes for the upper living areas, and it diminished the mass of the lower floor by concealing it into the shape of the dune. Utilities were contained in four masonry towers, which also housed the residence's four bathrooms.

The resulting structure, completed in 1966, was a dynamic composition of major-above-minor volumes. Emphasis was placed where it belonged, on the upper story, and Morgan's innovative design avoided the monotony of two equal stacked volumes. Morgan designed pivoting sunscreens, which were counterweighted to assist in their opening and closing. In their closed position the screens protected the glass walls of the house from the fierce sun, wind-blown debris during storms, and potential vandalism.

Morgan again broadcast photos and plans of his designs. The Williamson Residence was featured in *Architectural Record*, *Arts & Architecture*, *House and Garden*, *Maison Française*, and other publications. The house was designated one of the top one hundred buildings in Florida by the Florida Chapter of AIA.

Morgan's efforts at protecting the Williamson Residence from hurricanes preserved the building's interiors when Hurricane Matthew struck in October 2016, but the storm destroyed its beachfront porches and stairs, exposing its foundation. Hurricane Irma in September 2017 inflicted additional damage. The building was sited closer to the shore than neighboring structures, which were built after strict requirements for coastal construction were implemented in Florida, and this made it more vulnerable to violent storms and coastal erosion. It was demolished on October 26, 2017.

Above: Figure 42. Early sketch of Goodloe Residence. Courtesy of the William Morgan Collection, University of Florida Libraries.

Right: Figure 43. Goodloe Residence, terrace linking two of the eight building units. Courtesy of the William Morgan Collection, University of Florida Libraries.

Figure 44. Goodloe Residence, Ponte Vedra Beach, Florida. View from the west highlighting prefabricated modules in "pinwheel" formation. Courtesy of the William Morgan Collection, University of Florida Libraries.

For an oceanfront site in even more remote South Ponte Vedra Beach, Morgan designed a dramatic prefabricated house for George Goodloe. The building, completed in 1965, consisted of modular rectangles assembled in a pinwheel plan on the two upper stories of a three-story house, echoing a concept often deployed by his mentor Paul Rudolph. Jan Hochstim's 2004 volume *Florida Modern* features the striking Goodloe Residence on the cover.[7] George Goodloe had gone to high school with Morgan, graduated in the same class, and remained a lifelong friend.

This simple beach house provided an opportunity for Morgan to experiment. He designed eight prefabricated plywood boxes, each eight feet by twenty-four feet in length, which formed the upper two levels of the house. "Only three of the rectangles per floor are enclosed; the fourth becomes an open terrace. Because of the reverse rotation of the third floor around the core, however, the containers are not stacked, but are positioned 90 degrees to each other, creating voids and roof projections at all sides," noted Hochstim.[8]

The reverse direction of the spaces on alternating floors emphasized the interplay of light and shadows on the building's façades. Morgan's design responded to the harsh ocean environment. He coated the exterior surfaces of the modular units with the smooth white fiberglass resin used for boat hulls.

According to Morgan, the platforms were sized to be transported on public roads without escort. Problems arose, however, when the prefabricated modules were assembled on site—their weight required a crane. This and other unforeseen problems increased the cost of construction nearly to the level of conventional construction.

Goodloe considered the house quite livable and was pleased with the dramatic result. "It was a little experimental," he recalled. "The exterior was all fiberglass over plywood siding. As far as I know, that was the first time that had been done."

However, the isolation of South Ponte Vedra Beach proved an obstacle for his family. "After a few years, with small children, we were just too isolated. That was in the seventies," Goodloe said. "We sold it." The building was later resold and destroyed by its third owners, to be replaced by something larger and more predictable. It is one of three Morgan-designed houses to have been demolished as of the writing of this book. As noted, the nearby Williamson Residence experienced severe storm damage, which led to its demolition.

William Morgan's fascination with portable or prefabricated architecture extends from his earliest assignment at Harvard's Graduate School of Design—the Guam Vacation House. His reputation for inventiveness attracted clients who supported his experimentation, such as George Goodloe. One plug-in idea of his, though, never made it past the conceptual stage—the Interpod, an unusual idea and a lens providing a glimpse into Morgan's creative mind.

During his Wheelwright travels Morgan found himself repeatedly packing and unpacking his belongings. This inspired the architect. Instead of staying in a hotel, Morgan thought it made sense to design a portable dwelling that people could take with them throughout their travels and throughout their lives. The concept was not entirely new. Nomads have existed from prehistory well into the era of the modern recreational vehicle, but Morgan gave his units a space-age swagger.

Each pod would consist of an eight-foot by eight-foot self-contained living unit that could function independently or be plugged into other pods as well as into a multi-story structure that would house necessary utilities. Interpod included these utility towers as well as vehicles for transporting and assembling the prefabricated units into multiple-dwelling buildings. As Morgan conceived the project, the units would even be capable of being conveyed to remote locations by boat, helicopter, and blimp.

"Instead of putting your possessions in a suitcase and trying to go around the world for a month, you just lock the door and push some buttons, call a helicopter, and lift up with your unit," Morgan said. "George Goodloe's place in Ponte Vedra Beach was the start of Interpods," Morgan added. "That was the basic idea, except that they (the prefab units at the Goodloe Residence) were not movable."

36'
S
S
B
L
L+3BR
MULTI STORY TRAILER PARK
1965-66

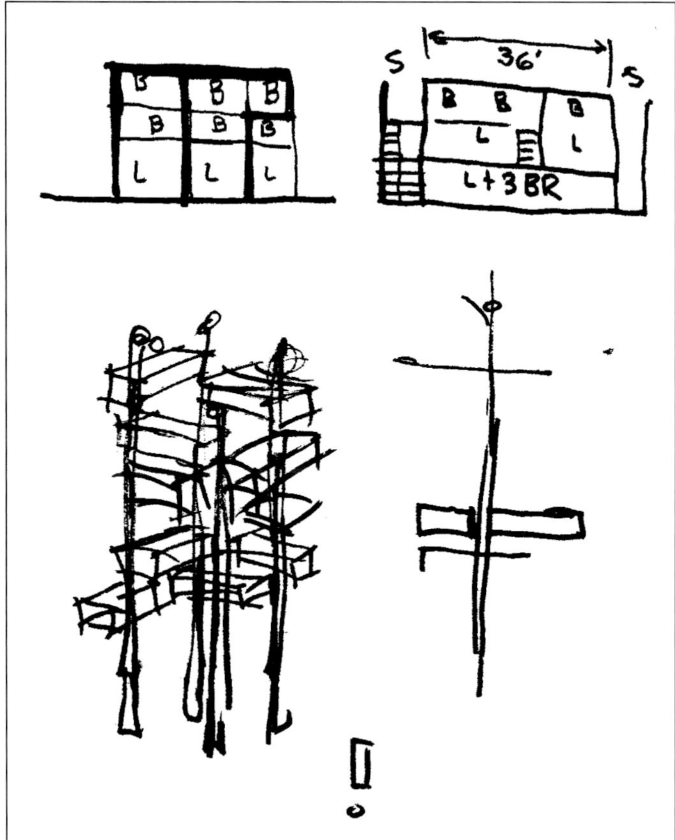

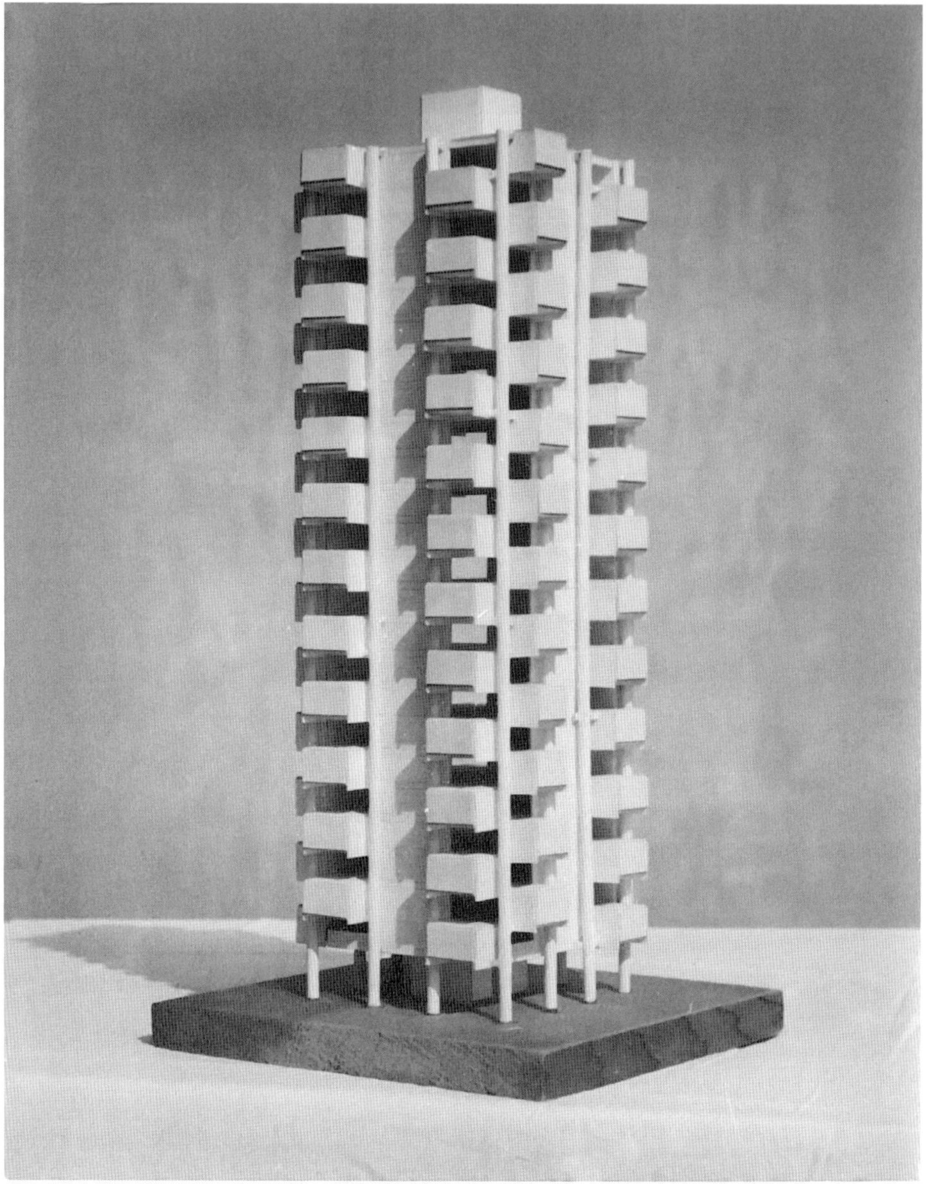

Facing page, left: Figure 45. Early drawing of a "multi-story trailer park," with prefabricated units arranged in a spiraling pinwheel arrangement around a central "tree" for services. Courtesy of the William Morgan Collection, University of Florida Libraries.

Facing page, right: Figure 46. Model of a residential deployment of the Interpod system. Courtesy of the William Morgan Collection, University of Florida Libraries.

Right: Figure 47. Stacked arrangement of Interpod design provides covered balconies under cantilevered living areas. Courtesy of the William Morgan Collection, University of Florida Libraries.

Not everyone shared his enthusiasm for a portable living pod. "People said, 'You're out of your mind,'" recalled Morgan. But Morgan never let a naysayer sway an unshakable belief in his own creative imagination. "I said, 'I'm very much in my mind,'" Morgan remembered.

At the time there was considerable interest in modular housing, including Moshe Safdie's well-known Habitat project featured at Expo 67, the World's Fair in Montreal, which remains a viable residential community. Paul Rudolph explored prefabricated, self-contained units in his Oriental Masonic Gardens project in New Haven, Connecticut. It was completed in 1971 but razed ten years later. Rudolph also experimented with high-rise groupings of prefabricated units in his Graphic Arts Center design for New York City in 1967.[9]

While they were never realized, the architectural community showed interest in Morgan's pods. The April 1967 issue of *Arts & Architecture* considered a wide range of modular responses to architecture and highlighted the portability aspect of Interpod.[10] The modular concept was also integral to a large urban development project in Norfolk, Virginia, that Morgan designed but that was never built.

Hurricane Aftermath

The arrival of Hurricane Dora in 1964 not only interfered with the only Beatles concert in Jacksonville's Gator Bowl; it also reshaped the oceanfront at the nearby beach communities. A long stretch of oceanfront was altered beyond recognition, and many millions of dollars' worth of buildings were lost as a result of the storm. For Morgan the hurricane presented opportunity, as its wave of destruction opened the door for new development and an array of brilliant projects.

The greatest concentration of William Morgan designs is in Atlantic Beach, Florida, his home for much of his life, where twenty-one projects include his first building at 1611 Ocean Boulevard; the Seaplace Condominium, completed in 1966; and projects in adjacent communities along the northeast Florida coastline. Constructed over several decades, these structures display a wide range of influences, including Le Corbusier's modernism and Florida vernacular architecture.

Morgan remembered that after Dora had passed, the U.S. Army Corps of Engineers, in cooperation with property holders and municipalities, installed a seawall of granite boulders along the oceanfront and restored much of the beach by pumping sand into the shoreline. Most of the beachfront property owners had assumed they would need to erect conventional bulkheads and fill in places where the violent surf had washed away the front of ancient dunes, leaving massive cliffs of sand.

However, despite this new protection of the shore against future hurricanes, many beachfront owners decided to get out, sell their properties at extremely low prices, and leave future development to others. Morgan took advantage of this opportunity. After Dora he bought three adjoining oceanfront properties for later development. The sites had been deemed a washout, essentially a cliff carved out of a dune by Hurricane Dora. Washouts were thought to be unsuitable for building upon in their present form, but Morgan looked at such sites and found in them an appealing design challenge.

Conventional developers and real estate people would be expected to fill in and then level such sites to ready them for construction. Morgan would later design buildings to accommodate the steep planes of the washout while respecting remaining portions of the dune, with minimal reshaping of the site to conform to the structures.

Not long after Dora struck, Morgan was presented with an opportunity to design a large multi-use project that potentially would change the commercial landscape of Atlantic Beach. The developers of what is now Seaplace Condominium asked him to design a project to replace the old Atlantic Beach Hotel, which had been damaged by the storm. The sprawling property had been a popular vacation destination since the turn of the twentieth century. Developers Jim Winston, Hugh Culverhouse, and associates bought a vacant portion of the hotel site following Hurricane Dora, and they asked Morgan to join their team and design something for the site. Completed in 1966, Seaplace gave Morgan his first large commission.

Figure 48. A courtyard in Seaplace (originally Place by the Sea), Atlantic Beach, Florida. The lagoons have been removed and the T1-11 plywood siding panels have been replaced with weather-resistant vinyl. Courtesy of the William Morgan Collection, University of Florida Libraries. Photo by Alexandre Georges.

Left: Figure 49. Aerial view of Seaplace, soon after construction, showing its orientation toward the Atlantic Ocean and the old Atlantic Beach Hotel. Courtesy of the William Morgan Collection, University of Florida Libraries. Photo by Alexandre Georges.

Above: Figure 50. Photo of William Morgan standing before drawing of the Place by the Sea, including the unrealized second phase between the one-hundred-unit apartment complex and the ocean. The second phase was to include a hotel, restaurant, pier, and tower. From the Morgan family.

He suggested a mid-rise, high-density, hundred-unit apartment complex suitable for future condominium ownership.

This project was the first one that Preston Haskell and his international design-build firm the Haskell Company (then known as Continental Construction Company) undertook. After hearing that developers Jim Winston and Hugh Culverhouse were planning the project, Haskell left his position with the S. S. Jacobs Company, where he had first worked on the Brundage Motors project. The Seaplace developers hired him in the summer of 1965 as construction manager, and he worked with Morgan on scoping, planning, scheduling, constructability, and drawing up a budget. According to Haskell, Jim Winston had a $1 million budget for the hundred-unit project, excluding such things as buying the land and architect's fees. "I was charged, among other things," Haskell noted, "with staying below budget. Bill [Morgan] was very good at achieving that."

To broaden their perspective, Morgan, Haskell, Winston, and developer Paul Fletcher flew in a small airplane to visit similar projects, particularly in Texas, where a boom in building garden apartments in the 1960s made it a center of advanced design and construction techniques. This fact-finding trip helped the team understand innovative ways to achieve density, to secure alternative financing, to work with building codes, and to overcome other constraints. These trips also provided the group an opportunity to brainstorm and develop ideas that Morgan would incorporate into the Seaplace project.

While Morgan was designing the complex, he also studied two garden apartments with interior courtyards in Chicago, designed by Frank Lloyd Wright between 1895 and 1901—the Francis Apartments and Lexington Terrace. Wright's designs grouped conventional apartments around central courtyards, which provided additional light and air while maintaining privacy. Morgan said he also studied the two-bedroom apartments designed by Le Corbusier for his Unité d'Habitation in Marseille in the late 1940s. Le Corbusier's design featured stacked bi-level apartments facing a central hallway on one side and living rooms with two-story interiors. Morgan's design combined the designs of Wright and Le Corbusier into a fresh and cheap-to-construct package. He created compact two-story spaces that faced either the street or the ocean as well as a landscaped central courtyard. Morgan noted that instead of having one large garden for all one hundred apartments of Seaplace, he created three more intimate gardens, each scaled to the apartments' dimensions.

Morgan's design consists of four precisely square building modules with thirty-eight living units facing the oceanfront, and sixty-two living units with ocean or inshore views. In all the project contained one-, two-, three-, and four-bedroom apartments, but Morgan believed the most impressive apartments were the two-bedroom units, which included two-story living rooms and wood-burning fireplaces. The apartment building featured included central courtyards, one with a swimming pool, one with entry drives and parking, and two with additional gardens accessible to everyone in the complex. Morgan's site plan provided ocean views from apartments as well as view corridors to the ocean from the street.

The developers named the project "Place by the Sea." It was later renamed "Seaplace," by which name it is presently known. Morgan remained proud of the project, recalling in his later years:

> What I had done was turn the building so they had views of the ocean that were diagonal, but pulled apart, and there were these through-views from Place by the Sea and from Ocean Boulevard. You could see right through the building to the oceanfront. It was damn good and the individual units were after Le Corbusier's Unité d'Habitation in Marseille, which was the prototype for the two-bedroom unit [on] the second and third floors. I designed it and Jim [Winston] asked, "Who are we going to get to build it?" It was light years ahead of anything that had been built that I knew of in Jacksonville. One of us asked, "What about that new kid over at S. S. Jacobs, Preston Haskell?"

Construction started in November 1965, Haskell remembered, and the first units were ready for occupancy in May 1966. The repetitiveness of the design made it economical and quick to build. Haskell was impressed then with the design, as he is now with the durability of the complex.

"The building is still standing today," Morgan said, "and unlike most fifty-year-old garden apartments, it's still in great shape. The fundamental design is intact, making wide use of concrete ribbon beams, buff brick, and T1-11 siding."

Morgan planned for generous views of the Atlantic from the garden apartments as part of the original plan for the complex, which included a motel, cabanas, restaurants, a bar atop a 120-foot tower, and a 600-foot pier extending into the Atlantic.[11] Those structures would

Right: Figure 51. A block-long wall, at right, now severs Seaplace from the beach. Photo by Brad Chesivoir.

Facing page: Figure 52. Planned view corridors to the Atlantic Ocean were never realized. Photo by the author.

TOW AWAY
ZONE

have filled in the property from the hundred-unit apartment complex to the ocean, but the design also preserved the apartments' ocean views. Instead, the old hotel remained on the site until it was torn down later in the 1960s. The developers had made substantial investments in repairing the hotel after the storm, which for the moment appeared to be prudent. Winston and Culverhouse later sold the property on which it stood, and the ambitious plan for the mixed-use development was abandoned.

A more conventional condominium project, the Cloister, now occupies the former hotel site to the east of Seaplace, from which it is abruptly separated by a wall. This later project destroyed the ocean views that were intrinsic to Morgan's original design for Seaplace.

Morgan considered Seaplace a "very important stepping stone" for his career, and he said he learned several lessons from Seaplace. It taught him the importance of the architect's participation in project planning at the earliest phase of design as well as the architect's responsibility for thorough design documentation. "These lessons were derived from experience, not from inspiration. They were learned on the job, not in the classroom," Morgan reflected. Seaplace garnered several design awards and was widely published in magazines, including *Architectural Record* and *House and Home.*

6

The Practice Expands

As the 1970s began Morgan embarked on a string of large projects in mostly urban settings. The vast scope and specialized functions of these projects differed from his previous work, which had been largely residential, and motivated him to develop further his tree system for designing large interior spaces and covered outdoor plazas. But in these buildings Morgan also amplified other themes that continued to occupy him, such as earth architecture and respect for building sites. He explored ways of expressing early architecture of the Americas in modern designs and with innovative use of materials.

With an expanding practice, Morgan moved in 1970 from 1611 Ocean Boulevard in Atlantic Beach to the high-rise Universal Marion Building in downtown Jacksonville. The additional space enabled the firm to hire a larger staff and to pursue large projects consistently. With the move Bunny Morgan commuted to the new office and worked full-time for the firm.

Work was Morgan's life, but Bunny enabled him to achieve success and recognition. "She was more than his biggest supporter," their son Dylan Morgan remembered. "She was the business mind, she was the accountant, the publicist—everything rolled up into one."

Those who worked with Morgan remember his ability to conceptualize projects, his discipline, and his perfectionism. "Morgan did very complete designs from the initial concepts, and then we would take it from there," said architect Tom McCrary, who worked with Morgan for fifteen years.

William Ebert, who worked for Morgan from 1973 to 1986, recalled a typical process for new projects:

> When he started a project he'd have Bunny do research for other buildings that were similar. They would maybe have Xeroxed copies or things he was thinking about for structural systems or things that might relate to the design. He'd have these articles on a desk across the aisle. He'd leave the stuff there for a couple of weeks while he'd be thinking about the project. Maybe that was the time the contract was being signed. Then he'd come into the office on Saturday. You'd come into the office Monday morning and, if you were going to be the guy working on the project, he'd sit down with you at 8:30 in the morning and he would have it all worked out with sketches for site plans, floor plans, exterior elevations, sections, building systems. He'd have everything figured out. You would never see it until he had it all worked out. To me it was remarkable that it wasn't just a germ of an idea—it was pretty much fully developed how everything fit together and everything worked.

Tom Duke, another architect who worked for Morgan, remembered Morgan's perfectionism:

> Bill had this zeal and enthusiasm for every project that would come in the door. He wanted to make it the absolute best. Someone once asked what he specialized in. He said, "I specialize in excellence—excellence in design." He would walk away from projects rather than compromising his standards of design.

Celebration was part of the firm's culture. The work week would end every Friday afternoon with "happy hour." Morgan's staff would come down for drinks, pretzels, and frequently a slide show, where Morgan would talk about a project or something that interested him. Independence Day was celebrated every year with a party at the Morgan Residence in Atlantic Beach.

For the life of the practice, Morgan remained keenly aware of early lessons learned on the value of publicity. The firm never advertised but promoted itself through journal articles around the world and entries into design competitions. After every project was completed, architectural photographers were hired to document the work properly. Architect and sculptor David Engdahl, who worked for Morgan, remembered the importance of promotion for the practice and Bunny Morgan's role in achieving it:

> Bunny was Bill's sidekick in the office and her job was to promote his work everywhere she could. Besides managing the office, Bunny was constantly sending stuff out for publication. And that's how she spent her day, every day, all day long. So, in a small office, Bill had a full-time PR person. I came to learn a lot about design, but I learned a heck of a lot more about promotion and about how to think.

The Jacksonville Children's Museum (now the Museum of Science and History) was Morgan's first major public building, and winning the commission was extremely important to him. Indeed, prior to his selection, Morgan had offers to work with numerous firms, including Eero Saarinen's in Michigan. Had he not been awarded the Children's Museum in 1968, he would have moved. The architect conceded that his selection was helped by his friendship with the head of the selection committee, George Varn, another Harvard man, whose Varn Trading Company owned many thousands of acres of southern yellow pine in southern Georgia and northeast Florida.

During the bid process Morgan formed a strong team of mechanical engineers, electrical engineers, and structural engineers—more than enough expertise to allay any fear of engaging a novice "who might do something dumb," as Morgan put it.

Morgan backed his proposal with extensive research. He visited many successful museums, including the Boston Children's Museum, as he prepared his submission. The hard work paid off. The committee chose Morgan.

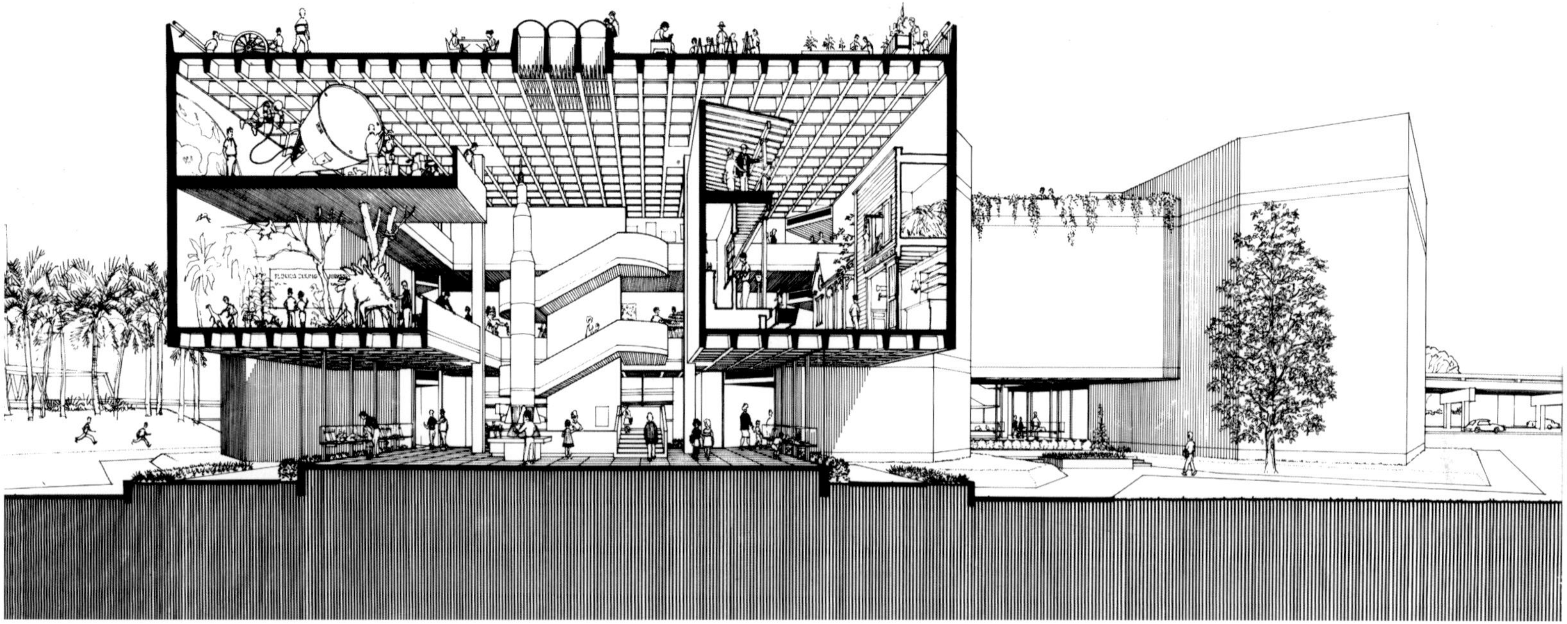

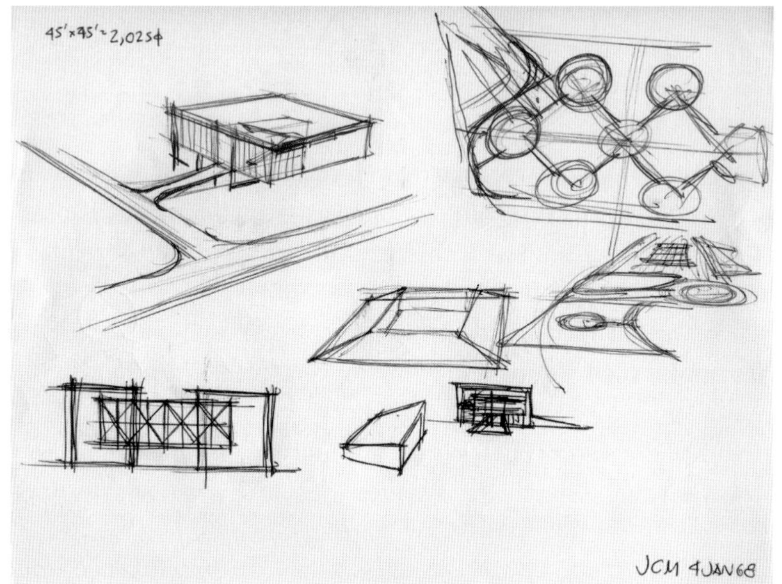

Facing page: Figure 53. Jacksonville Children's Museum. Main entrance between towers that dominate the design. Courtesy of the William Morgan Collection, University of Florida Libraries. Photo by Alexandre Georges.

Above: Figure 54. Jacksonville Children's Museum elevation. The original design included rooftop gardens and exhibit areas. Courtesy of the William Morgan Collection, University of Florida Libraries.

Left: Figure 55. Early sketches for Jacksonville Children's Museum. One design included access by a bridge traversing a moat—a concept Morgan later employed with his design for the Murray Hill Post Office in Jacksonville. Courtesy of the William Morgan Collection, University of Florida Libraries.

Facing page: Figure 56. View from the west of the Jacksonville Children's Museum, which is now identified as the Museum of Science and History. The forceful, poured-in-place towers are now obscured by palms and a protected walkway. Photo by Brad Chesivoir.

He designed the Jacksonville Children's Museum to be constructed in two phases. The initial phase called for powerful concrete towers on the western portion of the site. The second phase would have duplicated the spatial arrangement of the phase 1 towers. As ultimately executed, the second phase is a rectangular structure, which was an addition designed by a rival firm.

The towers included classrooms and individual work areas. An elevated level above the main entrance housed most of the exhibition space. The design also included a planetarium to the west, which is still in use in the Children's Museum's present incarnation.

The proximity of a nearby elevated expressway approaching the Main Street Bridge influenced his design, Morgan said. Given the expressway's noise, Morgan located the initial phase of the museum as far as possible to the west. Access to the museum was also oriented to the west, so as to avoid the danger that children might wander onto busy Main Street. Morgan's arrangement protected them from harm in a very congested area of the city that bordered an Interstate highway on one side and the St. Johns River on the other. The result is a building that in many ways speaks far less to its riverfront site than do Morgan's other waterfront projects. The architect described it as "a castle for the children" that would "protect them from an environment with wall-to-wall trucks and buses and all kinds of wheeled vehicles that can hurt young people."

William Morgan is best known for his work with earth architecture, an area of expertise that parallels his interest in archaeology. His research documented pre-Columbian earthen architecture in the United States, ranging from burial mounds to the vast array of mounds, terraces, and pyramids of the Cahokia complex, east of St. Louis.

For Morgan, earth architecture was a way to link contemporary buildings to the prehistory of their locations, a way to harmonize with nature, and a way to work economically with the peculiarities of building sites.

The Florida State Museum (now Dickinson Hall) on the University of Florida campus was William Morgan's first attempt at earth architecture as a professional architect.[1] Shortly after

MOSH
Museum Of Science & History

Facing page: Figure 57. View looking west, Florida State Museum (now Dickinson Hall), Gainesville, Florida. The treeless landscape in this early shot highlights the relationship of cascading terraces and platforms. Courtesy of the William Morgan Collection, University of Florida Libraries. Photo by Alexandre Georges.

designing the Children's Museum in Jacksonville, Morgan was asked to design the new natural history museum on the campus of the University of Florida in Gainesville. Jacksonville architect Forrest Kelley, who was the advisor to the State Board of Regents, was given the job of identifying architects for this project and he recommended Morgan, the only architect in Florida who had recently completed a large museum in the state—the Jacksonville Children's Museum.

During the early stages of the project's design, Morgan visited department heads to see what they wanted. Ripley P. Bullen, then curator of anthropology and chairman of the University's Department of Social Sciences, and whom Morgan regarded as a "museum piece himself," had a drawing on his cluttered desk of a truncated pyramid with an extended ramp. When the architect remarked upon the drawing, Bullen noted that it was located just a few miles away from the museum site. As we have seen, Morgan's interest in earth architecture dated back to his years as an architecture student at Harvard and was later enhanced during his Wheelwright travel. "I was elated at seeing this drawing," Morgan said. The following weekend the architect packed his wife and boys up in their Chevrolet station wagon and headed down to see the prehistoric mound.[2]

The visit to the archaeological site was a revelation to the architect: "The sloping walls on that earth pyramid on Ripley Bullen's desk I took almost as a mandate not to hesitate, but to go straight in on earth building—and not to build it as a basement space, but build it in huge volumes, which is what the museum needed."

The new project was to be built on a hillside at the corner of two busy streets near the center of the campus. "I began to develop ideas that had multiple terraces. Each would possess different exhibits, and these exhibits would change," Morgan said. "There would be pyramids and there would be terraces incorporated into the museum's design. In view of the Florida State Museum's interest in the pre-Columbian, earth seemed a most useful material." Morgan also believed that the "jumbled site of two nearby buildings and the proximity of the streets and so forth suggested it would be nice to do something very quiet at that site."

Left: Figure 58. Florida State Museum (now Dickinson Hall), view looking west along Museum Drive highlighting vine-covered berm and concrete roof panels, the latter of which have since been replaced with metal units. Courtesy of the William Morgan Collection, University of Florida Libraries. Photo by Alexandre Georges.

Above: Figure 59. William Morgan with a model of the Florida State Museum. Courtesy of the William Morgan Collection, University of Florida Libraries.

Morgan and Florida State Museum director J. C. Dickinson Jr. visited similar museums in the Northeast and interviewed the directors of several of the museums, hoping to gain some inspiration for the new building's design:

> We traveled together to gather information, brochures, and documentation of every description for several months. During the evenings, we compared the day's experiences and discussed items to be included and those to be discarded from the new museum's program. Of particular interest to me were economical construction techniques and ease of future expansion. Printed information was carefully assembled and annotated each evening and filed in black leather file-cases measuring approximately nine-by-twelve inches by ten or twelve inches high. The sources of the cases were unknown to me, but I noticed that one empty case carried easily six or eight bottles of the finest available gin, together with appropriate tonic. Dr. Dickinson proved to be an expert unexcelled in the field of museum planning every evening. A man with an open mind. Wide open.

Morgan's inspiration for the Florida State Museum's unique interplay of platforms and plazas came from carefully observing the museum site on the University of Florida campus.

> Finally, I went to the site and watched it quietly. First of all, I noticed a steady stream of students moving diagonally across the site between academic buildings to the northeast and to the southwest. The new museum should not block the stream of students; it should facilitate that as well as informing them of current exhibits, perhaps through the use of window displays along the way. Service vehicles would be confined to the site's southeast and northwest corners. The museum's main exhibition halls were to be as free of columns and partitions as possible—and the museum's collection of artifacts would be directly available to researchers on the lower levels. A courtyard with exhibitions would be located to the southwest. The site proved to be a valuable determinant of the new museum's design.

Facing page: Figure 60. Florida State Museum (now Dickinson Hall). Contemporary view showing interplay of terraces and walkways. The earthen berm at left is partly concealed by a southern magnolia. Photo by Brad Chesivoir.

The building enchanted architecture critic Wolf von Eckardt, who compared it to Aztec, Mayan, and Cambodian "temple cities that are similarly carved into hillsides." Von Eckardt's 1972 description of the complex remains apt to this day: "You enter the grassy mound through a tunnel," he wrote, "and find yourself on the museum's upper level, overlooking an enchanting labyrinth of interlocking sculpture courts and earth mounds. The courts are connected by tunnels and bridges and framed on two sides with terraced gardens."[3]

The museum's construction process created a gigantic berm, which informed Morgan's design and remains visible today along Museum Road as part of the finished building. Earth was used to create the upper exhibition level of the museum. Down the hill, on various levels, were research facilities.

The north-facing side of the building featured sloping, prestressed concrete slabs that formed a roofline along the top of the berm and elsewhere. Through a structural engineering error, the panels had a weight that exceeded the capacity of the bearing points, which resulted in spalling, an indicator of early failure and collapse. Areas of the museum that had the overhead shelter detail were promptly closed off, and the concrete panels were replaced with lightweight metal roofs.

The wide use of platforms and terraces alluded to Native American communities, which were among the principal subjects of the museum.

Morgan recalled:

> The nature of the site and the nature of the building are one, and the intention was to enhance the strength of the site with the building. The terraces are intended to become rooms, open to the sky, but rooms nonetheless in their plan relationships to the interior spaces of the museum.

The building was designed to be both cost-effective and efficient in its use of space. Dickinson was pleased with the result: "Operationally, it's the most economical building on the entire

Left: Figure 61. Contemporary view of Florida State Museum (now Dickinson Hall). The terraces remain, as designed, a quiet place to relax, although the original spatial array is somewhat concealed by more than forty-five years of tree growth. Photo by Brad Chesivoir.

Above: Figure 62. Contemporary view of stairs up earthen berm, leading to elevated walkway on grounds of former Florida State Museum. The pyramidal shape and stairs flanked by *alfardas* are reminiscent of Mesoamerican themes. Photo by Brad Chesivoir.

Facing page: Figure 63. William Morgan Residence, Atlantic Beach, Florida. View from the south highlighting the topography generated by the washout during Hurricane Dora. Properties to the south of the house have all since been developed, including the Dunehouses next door. Courtesy of the William Morgan Collection, University of Florida Libraries. Photo by Ronald Thomas.

campus," he said shortly after it opened. The $2.1 million building was completed in 1971 and cost only $21 per square foot. It remains one of Morgan's best-known buildings.

The academic interests of Bullen and Dickinson shaped the design of the facility but also fed Morgan's interest in early architecture. Bullen and Dickinson passed information on pre-Columbian sites to the architect and introduced him to other archaeology scholars.

As Morgan's work evolved, the nature of building sites had more influence on his designs. His own house in Atlantic Beach, completed in 1972, mimics the topography of a lofty dune through the use of a triangular structure containing four platforms, which descend along the washout. An unbroken sloping roof encloses the four platforms. Large east-facing windows and a narrower clerestory provide generous natural light for the interiors. Exterior surfaces are entirely covered with natural-finished cedar siding and cedar-shake roofing.

Large beams along the building's spines provide its structural support. A narrow staircase leads from the street-level foyer to an open master bedroom and studio area on the uppermost platform. This level is a large loft spanning the width of the building.

An open first floor includes the living room, dining room, and kitchen—all with dramatic views of the Atlantic from their elevated position. Doorways from the living and dining rooms provide access to two ocean-facing balconies. These areas surround a broad central staircase, which is flanked by two small bedrooms on opposite sides of the stairs on the third platform from the top. On the lowest level, opposing open beach rooms containing a Ping-Pong table and storage for surfboards, small watercraft, and other beach equipment can be found. The natural cedar exterior of the residence forges a dramatic contrast to the surfaces of the buildings flanking it, also designed by Morgan—the Dylan Morgan Residence to the north and the Dunehouses to the south.

Over the years the Morgan Residence was featured in many publications, including *Architectural Record* and the *AIA Journal*. *Playboy* magazine included an article on the Morgan family house entitled "Playboy Pad on the Beach" in its August 1975 edition.[4]

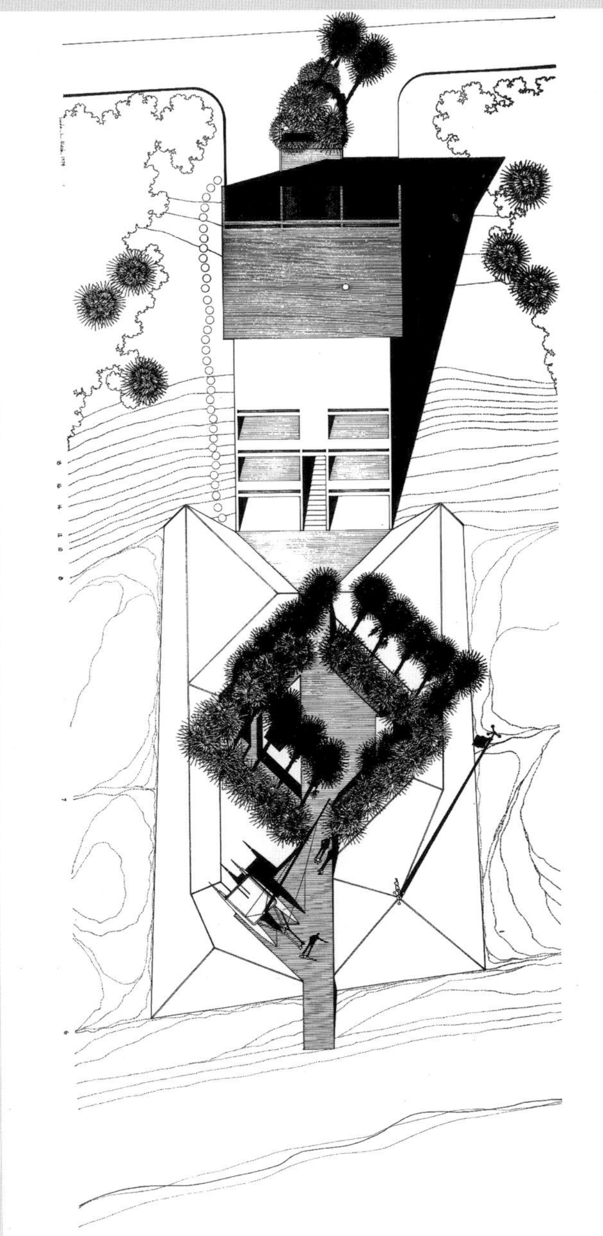

Facing page, left: Figure 64. William Morgan Residence, Atlantic Beach, Florida. Site plan highlights steep contours descending from the top of the dune to the bottom of the washout. Courtesy of the William Morgan Collection, University of Florida Libraries.

Facing page, right: Figure 65. Interior of William Morgan Residence. The open layout on the uppermost levels offers spectacular ocean views, maximizing the benefit of the elevated building site. Clerestory windows above offer indirect lighting during the day, while avoiding the intense heat of Florida's afternoon sun. Courtesy of the William Morgan Collection, University of Florida Libraries. Photo by Alexandre Georges.

Left: Figure 66. Bunny and William Morgan in an early view of the garden beneath their residence. Courtesy of the William Morgan Collection, University of Florida Libraries.

Left: Figure 67. Contemporary view from the beach framed by two palms. The two open rooms on ground level were designed to accommodate small boats and beach paraphernalia. Photo by Brad Chesivoir.

Above: Figure 68. Contemporary view of the garden. Deck and furnishings have changed little over the years, but the dune structure between the garden and the beach has generally increased. Photo by Brad Chesivoir.

In February 1972 Morgan not only moved into his new residence in Atlantic Beach but also relocated his offices to a former livery stable building at 1611 Forsyth Street in downtown Jacksonville, which he had purchased and repurposed for offices. The principal work space was uncluttered, open, and orderly, with ten built-in desks occupying two rows. Morgan occupied a desk in the rear.

For the two-story Dickinson Residence on the Atlantic Beach oceanfront, completed in 1973, Morgan designed a lower floor partly recessed into an ancient dune crest, with a larger second floor cantilevered out on all four sides. Placed in the middle of its site, the structure has a commanding presence, which Morgan said echoed the Governor's Palace at Uxmal, a Mayan site on the Yucatán Peninsula. Indeed, the inspiration was so potent that upon agreeing to design the house, Morgan loaned the nineteenth-century book *Incidents of Travel in Yucatan*, by John L. Stephens, to his clients and urged them to visit Uxmal. Maxwell and Edna Dickinson complied. "We flew into Mérida in the Yucatán and drove out to Uxmal, and then we went back to Mérida and went to Chichén Itzá, then hopped a plane to Cozumel," Edna recalled.

The beachfront property had originally been purchased as an investment by the Dickinsons in 1956, and the family lived in an old wood-frame bungalow—basically what had once been a summer house—on the site. The Dickinsons were motivated to replace the older house by an Army Corps of Engineers project that thenceforth protected the property from the ravages of hurricanes, like Dora, with a barrier consisting of what Edna Dickinson described as "boulders the size of refrigerators." They also wanted to build a new house while their three children—then aged ten, twelve, and fourteen, were "were still young enough to enjoy it."

The site included the dune crest about one hundred feet west of the bulkhead along its eastern edge. The Dickinson House looks out over the dunes toward the broad expanse of the Atlantic Ocean. The focus and openness to the Atlantic energize the building's interior. West-facing lower-floor windows provide unbroken views of a relatively unadorned but private lawn.

Above: Figure 69. View from west of the Dickinson Residence. Courtesy of the William Morgan Collection, University of Florida Libraries. Photo by Alexandre Georges.

Facing page: Figure 70. Dickinson Residence. Dramatic view from the east (beach side) at night. Courtesy of the William Morgan Collection, University of Florida Libraries. Photo by Alexandre Georges.

Right: Figure 71. The Palace of the Governors, Uxmal, Yucatán. Morgan modeled the Dickinson Residence on the Maya ruin, and while it was being planned, he encouraged the Dickinsons to visit the site. The couple complied. Photo by the author.

Below: Figure 72. Preliminary sketch of the Dickinson Residence on a restaurant placemat. The original concept was largely executed. Courtesy of Edna and Maxwell Dickinson.

Earthen berms enclose the lower mass of the house, while the wood-framed upper floor and roof augment the volume of the upper mass and provide a counterbalance to the light and airy appearance of the first floor. While the Rawls House is freestanding on a relatively flat site, recessing the Dickinson House into the dune allows the upper floor mass to dominate the surrounding site much in the way that the Governor's Palace at Uxmal dominates its vicinity.

The Dickinson Residence is probably the simplest structure that Morgan ever designed. It consists of unbroken two-by-twelve wooden floor and ceiling joists, which rest on north-to-south spanning wood beams. Conventional wood studs and exterior siding enclose the upper floor. The structure's north and south walls are unbroken on both floors to provide added structural resistance to wind. A ceramic-tiled central space and an exterior terrace reminiscent of Mesoamerican themes form the heart of the plan. Living, dining, and entertaining spaces radiate from the building's central space.

Typical of Morgan residences, original building material and finishes were selected with the goal of maintaining a low cost, providing for minimal maintenance, and ensuring ease of replacement. The T1-11 siding that originally covered exterior walls, however, failed to stand up to the salt air and fierce storms on the beach. The siding has since been replaced with cedar shingles, but the house retains its simple beauty today.

During this period an official involved in building an amphitheater in Miami remembered Morgan's design for a floating canopy over an earthen bowl, which Morgan designed during his Fulbright travel and published in *L'Architettura*. He asked Morgan to create a similar canopied bowl for Miami's Interama, a proposed international trade fair on Biscayne Bay. "That was an international business fair proposed for Miami, put forward as a possibility for stimulating trade between Latin America and the U.S.," Morgan said. "Ideas were exchanged and it failed, but in the process of it going down the tubes, all the big guys in the United States, all the foremost architects, Lou Kahn and Paul Rudolph, for instance, submitted proposals.

Facing page: Figure 73. Contemporary view of Dickinson Residence. T1-11 plywood panels have been replaced with wooden shingles. Photo by Brad Chesivoir.

Above: Figure 74. The pattern of steps and terraces is reminiscent of pre-Columbian building and provides protection from storms. The dune in the background was largely erased by Hurricane Matthew in October 2016. Photo by Brad Chesivoir.

You just name the names. The most advanced thinking in the U.S. was going into a project of some kind at Interama, and ours was—huge."

Morgan brought in a leading international expert on tensile structures to work with him on the design. Horst Berger had already become well known for a tensile-roof design for the United States Pavilion at the 1968 Osaka World's Fair. He would later become famous for tensile structures at Denver International Airport in Colorado and King Fahd International Stadium in Riyadh, Saudi Arabia, among others.[5] "Together, we designed what would have been the world's largest tensile roof," Morgan recounted. "Unfortunately, the bond issue to build Interama failed, and the great tent remains unrealized," Morgan added. The entire Interama project was abandoned in 1975.

Sculptor and architect David Engdahl worked on the Interama project. Engdahl recalled how innovative Morgan's proposal was: "The concept on that project was no regular geometry. Every aspect of that project was irregular geometry. It was an interesting concept. We can do that now, but back then you had to hand-draw everything. It had what would have been the largest tensile-structure roof in the world," Engdahl said. "I don't know how many models we made using ladies' stretch-girdle material. We stretched the material on the models and Horst was amazed that that's how it would really work. The amphitheater design got published on the cover of *Architectural Record*."

Morgan recognized a critical problem with his design—preventing interlopers from climbing up the hillside and slipping into the amphitheater without paying for tickets. He laughingly recalled his solution: "To fix this problem without resorting to barbed wire fencing, I suggested a moat around the amphitheater's base," he said. "Bridges would accommodate ticket holders, and the moat would be filled with hungry alligators and water moccasins to discourage freeloaders."

7

Trailblazing in Earth Architecture

For William Morgan 1975 proved an important year. The American Institute of Architects elected him a Fellow, that organization's highest honor. The year also marked the completion of the Dunehouses in Atlantic Beach, Florida—an earth project that more than forty years later continues regularly to receive international attention. That Morgan would commit a valuable oceanfront lot to this unorthodox experiment attests to the architect's creativity and conviction.

On the oceanfront properties to the north and south of his own house, Morgan saw an opportunity to experiment with a new architecture for the oceanfront that would use the topography of the beach and dunes as a starting point in design. As it evolved, only the property to the south was dedicated to such an experiment, but it was one that attracted more attention than any other project from his career.

For the Dunehouses, Morgan extended his interest in earth architecture to apartment living. He designed two egg-shaped concrete shells that share a common party wall. The two-and-one-half-inch-thick concrete shells are buried into the same steep dune washout into which Morgan's own residence was constructed. Each apartment contains one bedroom and a single bath in a loft arrangement above the living, dining, and kitchen areas on the lower floor—that is to say, at beach level. Side-yard setbacks restricted the gross apartment width to

Facing page, left: Figure 75. Early view of the Dunehouses, Atlantic Beach, Florida. Like the Morgan Residence immediately to the north, the Dunehouses respect and highlight the contour of the dune. Courtesy of the William Morgan Collection, University of Florida Libraries. Photo by Creative Photo Service.

Facing page, right: Figure 76. Interior of Dunehouses highlighting Gunite surfaces on walls and ceilings, contrasting natural wood surfaces, dramatic lighting, and built-in furnishings. Courtesy of the William Morgan Collection, University of Florida Libraries. Photo by Alexandre Georges.

Left: Figure 77. Another early photo of the Dunehouses showing orientation toward the William Morgan House to the north. When first built, entrances from the beach were simple concrete openings emerging from the turf. Courtesy of the William Morgan Collection, University of Florida Libraries. Photo by Alexandre Georges.

approximately seventeen feet for each unit. Each apartment is of sufficient height inside to afford vertical clearances for two levels at the centers. According to Morgan, the grassy exterior above the concrete shells rose to the height of foliage on the original dune before Hurricane Dora struck.

The site was designed in such a way that the ground-floor slabs, utilities, and common wall would follow a continuous curve from the lower level. Around the perimeter, the skeleton of the structure is built by 3/8-inch-diameter steel reinforcing rebar, oriented vertically, with the bars about eight inches from one another. "I bent the bars over toward each other until they formed a basket-like shape with intersections above the floor, according to measurements supplied by the project engineer, Horst Berger," Morgan remembered. Over this basketwork were sheets of steel reinforced with stamped apertures large enough to permit Gunite concrete to be applied on both sides. The final Gunite surfaces formed walls and ceilings.

Within each of the two "eggs" Morgan built the loft, stairs, and millwork needed to create an apartment. Exterior stairs lead down from the street level to a common landing and the entry to the units: 1941 and 1943 Beach Avenue. From the landing one enters a short hall leading to the north and south bedroom and bath or proceeds down the curving stairs to the living and dining areas on the lower level. To the east a single large glass window and sliding door looks out across the dunes and beach to the Atlantic Ocean. The multi-level design renders the 750-square-foot units livable and surprisingly spacious.

Morgan said the temperature inside the Dunehouses corresponds closely to the temperature of groundwater around the site, which keeps cooling and heating costs down. Morgan believed the low initial costs and minimal expense of heating and cooling, as well as the use of low-maintenance Gunite, suggested such a technology could easily have wider application and acceptance. He viewed the sustainable technology of the Dunehouses as applicable to other purposes, such as student housing, holiday housing, or year-round communities.

Although the Dunehouses never took off as a new kind of apartment living, Morgan's modest experiment in low-cost housing insulated by the earth garnered international attention. The Dunehouses were at once amusing and technologically advanced. *Playboy* magazine featured the Dunehouses in its February 1977 issue under the headline, "Return of the Cave Man." The Dunehouses have also appeared in numerous professional journals, newspapers, and magazines nationally and internationally. They are regularly featured in television segments on green architecture and unusual design, including recent television programs that aired in France, Japan, and the United States.

In the context of Morgan's evolution as an architect, one might view the Dunehouses as a dead end. However, the architect himself viewed his best-known project as an adventure and still believed forty years later that they had potential for wider application: "It was discovery," he said. "The Dunehouses were very experimental, and they had great potential. We tried to carry the potential farther. We could establish a floor for two Dunehouses built side by side, and we imagined you could build another one atop the two lower ones—a sort of pyramidal shape."

Morgan had used spray-on Gunite before on the E.L.K. Oil Company Building in 1964. In the Dunehouses he expanded the application of Gunite by taking advantage of its flexibility to create the egg shapes. Morgan created the basket frame, covered it with metal sheeting, and then blew the Gunite onto it. Gunite creates a strong material when dry and it sets up quickly. "Those two characteristics make it possible to create woven-wire metal sculptures and then spray-apply concrete as if you were building a swimming pool—a Gunite pool," said Morgan in 2015. "It's the same basic idea, but having gone through the process, it occurs to me there's much more opportunity and availability of ideas and things we can be doing with Gunite in creating architecture. That's what the Dunehouses are all about. You can build a tube, for example, in the earth, a cave, a tunnel. It's perfect. That is what it was born to do."

Morgan admitted there are challenges using Gunite in building construction, but he did not think they were insurmountable:

> We had some very incidental use of Gunite prior to the Dunehouses. We tried it with this hanging structure.[1] We did it there. But you can't dawdle. If you take too much time, and you're adding so much weight to the structure, then you begin to get separation of the steel reinforcing. The steel stretches and the balance you're trying to get between tensile steel and compressive concrete is destroyed. The concrete will accumulate in such quantities that it becomes very heavy, and as it becomes heavy the weight begins to draw down by gravity the steel, and it distends and distorts the steel—and that's not good. You like to have steel in a structure where it belongs.

The thin egg shape that Morgan employed for the Dunehouses used the natural pressure from the earth pressing in equally on all sides of the buried egg shape to strengthen the structure:

> An egg works very much the same way, with a very thin shell and a careful balance. Once you crack that shell, then, of course, the whole thing is destroyed. You could build within the Earth and create peanut shapes from these interior shells. You can imagine all kinds of shapes. In the case of the Dunehouses, it's all integral—it's an egg. The combination of reinforcing steel and the positioning of steel and the positioning of very exotic, technologically advanced formwork—seeing the two things put together is what underlies it. These lumps of earth, these volumes we were building were very simple—the simplest of structures. They were simple, but they made a great deal of sense.

The Dunehouses were Morgan's first experience working with computers. The project also relied on the services of structural engineer Horst Berger, who had contributed to the unbuilt Interama project. Berger and his associates performed the structural engineering and analysis for the Dunehouses' eggs. "We had to invent a whole new way of placing steel—and holding it in place and doing it economically," Morgan related. "Horst was, fortunately, a very experimental-minded German, and he had a European attitude toward experimentation. They are very good about that."

HABITAT

RETURN OF THE CAVE MAN

As we all know, man's earliest choice for shelter was probably a nice cozy cave. *Plus ça change, plus c'est la même chose.* Today, man has again picked up on the idea, as witness this pair of mirror-image bachelor beach houses that architect William Morgan recently had carved into dunes at Atlantic Beach, Florida. Each of the twin pads is constructed of Gunite, a smooth, stone-free concrete that's shot from a gun into a mold. And because each of the sliding-door oceanside entrances has a massive expanse of glass, the air-conditioned 750-square-foot interiors are literally washed with light, the upstairs being an open bedroom balcony overlooking the living room. Most of the pad's furnishings are built in; behind the L-shaped living-room couch is a full-sized kitchen, plus a washer-drier. Interior acoustics are perfect for a hi-fi and, yes, there's wall-to-wall carpeting for shoes-off loafing. Furthermore, mother earth acts as a natural insulator, keeping the rooms cool in summer and warm in winter (they're electrically heated besides). And now the price: about $25,000 per unit. Head for the sand hills!

Behind each of the oceanside entrances, shown above, awaits a plush living room and kitchen, seen above right. The stairway leads to the bedroom balcony—a portion of which is shown below left. Below right: Two views of the pad's rear (front?) entrance, including a private terrace.

PHOTOGRAPHY BY BILL MARIS

Figure 78. "Return of the Cave Man." Archival material from *Playboy* magazine.

Right: Figure 79. Model of twenty-eight-student underground dwelling unit designed for and proposed to the University of West Florida, Pensacola, Florida. Courtesy of the William Morgan Collection, University of Florida Libraries.

Facing page: Figure 80. The Dunehouses viewed from the northeast after modifications by new owners and after a heavy storm in 2015, which resulted in flooding and a landslide, visible here. Photo by Brad Chesivoir.

Since Dunehouses offered economical construction, Morgan boasted that he could build Dunehouses to provide cheap housing for the State University System of Florida. He proposed building an experimental group of student housing units for the University of West Florida in Pensacola, but the school's administration was not persuaded. "It scared the bureaucrats to death," Morgan recalled.

The Morgans owned the Dunehouses and rented them out until 2012, when they sold them for $900,000. The new owners implemented major changes to landscaping and the interiors, significantly altering what had remained largely intact over the previous thirty-seven years.

Facing page: Figure 81. Exterior view of Hilltop House, near Brooksville, Florida. The site offers a view of five different Florida counties. Courtesy of the William Morgan Collection, University of Florida Libraries. Photo by Creative Photo Service.

Morgan created another striking example of earth architecture—this time in central Florida. In a rural area near Brooksville, the Hilltop House on Hickory Hill—completed in 1975—elegantly combines earth architecture with the pyramid motif of early American builders. Morgan wrote about such architecture in two of the five books he published during his lifetime, and he made use of pyramidal design in several of the works examined here as well as with the Forest House in Gainesville, Florida. Although the Hilltop House is one of Morgan's best-known buildings, he was initially disinterested in the commission.

Celebrating the completion of the Florida State Museum was a joyful occasion for Morgan. Notable persons from Tallahassee, Jacksonville, Gainesville, and many other parts of Florida were on hand. At one point Morgan excused himself to use the men's room, he remembered. An older gentleman with a kindly countenance using another urinal asked, "You're the architect, aren't you?"

"Why yes, I am," Morgan answered. The man made several complimentary observations about the museum and then asked, "Would you design a house for me?" He handed Morgan his business card, which identified him as Wayne Thomas. Morgan explained that he was in the middle of several large commissions, and he did not have time to undertake a private residence.

"I was not that busy," Morgan admitted later, "but I was trying to move beyond being only a designer of houses." Upon returning to his Jacksonville office, Morgan received an irate phone call from Florida State Museum director J. C. Dickinson.

"Morgan, do you remember that I told you that a certain person had given the money to build the museum?" Morgan recalled Dickinson saying.

"Why yes," he answered.

"If an elderly gentleman asks you to design a house for him, you should show him every consideration," Dickinson replied. Then he abruptly ended the call. Thomas, with large mining and real estate operations in central Florida and overseas, had donated a large sum of

Facing page: Figure 82. Model of Hilltop House. The lower level includes terraces on three sides of the pyramid. The fourth side, to the east, includes a driveway entrance and exit, along with a carport built into the earthen berm. Courtesy of the William Morgan Collection, University of Florida Libraries.

Left: Figure 83. Interior view of Thomas Residence's top-floor observatory, with spectacular views of the surrounding countryside. Morgan's elderly client would access the observatory by elevator in the morning and remain there until night. Courtesy of the William Morgan Collection, University of Florida Libraries. Photo by Creative Photo Service.

Facing page: Figure 84. Contemporary photograph of the Hilltop House, near Brooksville, Florida. The grass that originally covered the pyramidal berm has been replaced with dwarf confederate jasmine, which is easier to maintain. Photo by the author.

money for the new museum as well as parts of his own collections, which included fossil mammals discovered at his Bone Valley holdings in Polk County.

Morgan telephoned Thomas immediately. "My schedule has cleared up unexpectedly, Mr. Thomas," Morgan recalled telling him. "I'm able to undertake the design of your house immediately. Could I meet you tomorrow morning in Brooksville?"

Thomas's grandson remembers the story a bit differently. After Morgan proclaimed, "I don't build houses, never have built a house, and wouldn't consider it," Wayne Thomas repeated his request.

His interest piqued, Morgan asked, "But if I was to build a house, how big is the lot?" After Thomas told him it was three thousand acres, the architect reportedly became intrigued.

"We'll have a helicopter come up and fly you to the site," Thomas's grandson recalled his grandfather saying.

Morgan was impressed by the breathtaking hilltop site of the Thomas property, with what may be the only 360-degree hilltop view in Florida. From the top of the hill one can see five Florida counties: Hernando, Citrus, Pasco, Polk, and Sumter. "Mr. Wayne was here with his old clothes and his beat-up old Buick," said his grandson, "and when Morgan landed it was like 'I've got to do it.'"

The resulting Hilltop House is a freestanding pyramid built on the summit of a hill. From the pyramid's base one enters a central foyer that provides access to stairs and an elevator to a second-floor observatory with views in all directions. "From this space," said Morgan in a 1978 interview, "230 feet above the citrus groves below, it is possible to watch seven thunderstorms simultaneously in progress all over the horizon."[2] The elevator was an important feature for Morgan's eighty-five-year-old client, who typically would ascend to the second-story aerie in the morning and remain there into the night.

Thomas proved to be an excellent client for Morgan, making no demand on the architect other than, "I want it to blend into the surroundings." That requirement fit perfectly with Morgan's design principles. Morgan himself was pleased with the result.

Figure 85. View from the northeast showing main entrance and vehicular access. Photo by the author.

After Thomas's death in 1986 the house remained vacant for three years. Without heat or air conditioning, the building suffered serious mold and water damage, his grandson remembered. But subsequent investments over the years have returned Hilltop House to a source of pride for the family.

8

Bold Design on a Large Scale

In the late 1950s Jacksonville began a surge of public improvements, which sought to alter the city's image and quality of life. Talented architects, such as California's Welton Becket and Associates, reshaped the city's skyline. Local firm Hardwick and Lee designed an eccentric yet functional new public library and the riverfront Dallas Thomas Park, which included the city's well-known Friendship Fountain. Both facilities opened in 1965. With consolidation of the Jacksonville and Duval County governments in 1968, the city had become the largest in land area in the lower forty-eight states. Consistent with its newly adopted tagline "The Bold New City of the South," Jacksonville strove to continue aggressive public works projects, with some success.[1]

In 1971 the City of Jacksonville held an open design competition, sponsored by the American Institute of Architects, to select an architect for its new police administration building. This procedure was unprecedented in the history of a city where important architectural commissions previously were not awarded on the basis of an architect's design ability but on the basis of political patronage.

Morgan credited architect Herschel Shepard for creating this precedent:

Facing page: Figure 86. Early photo of the Police Memorial Building, highlighting landscaped terraces and bush-hammered concrete surfaces. Courtesy of the William Morgan Collection, University of Florida Libraries. Photo by Alexandre Georges.

> Herschel—I don't know how—was appointed professional advisor. Well, Jacksonville commissioners didn't need any architectural advice. They were architectural authorities. Jim Beam was their trusted advisor. At any rate, Herschel set up this competition using national AIA and international standards for competition but limiting the area to northeast Florida. You had to be a registered architect in northeast Florida to enter it, which quieted down the political opposition.

A panel of three distinguished professionals was invited to judge the competition entries, and the judges quickly agreed on the winner. Morgan's innovative concept prevailed. His design featured his "tree system" for constructing large interior spaces with multi-story vertical concrete shafts and radiating cantilevered supporting branches, and it included a rooftop public park—foreshadowing green roofs, which have become increasingly popular in the twenty-first-century push for sustainability.

Morgan extended his earth architecture concepts by adroitly fitting this large building into its site's topography. The building has a maximum height of four stories spread over its two blocks, and its terraced roof was intended to provide a gathering spot with views of the city and the St. Johns River amid an expected profusion of high-rise buildings in the city's downtown.

The Police Memorial Building boasted dramatic arrays of stairs and platforms, highly reminiscent of early monumental architecture in North America and Mexico. In a similar vein, Morgan described the building's tiered interior atria as resembling "inverted pyramids of space."[2] According to Morgan, one of the jurors, Joe Amisano, commenting on the speed with which the jury had made its decision, reported that selecting his entry was "like shooting fish in a barrel" in comparison with what others submitted.

Morgan's selection significantly enhanced his professional reputation. For the first time he had won a major architectural commission. Without hesitation, he assembled a team

Above: Figure 87. Police Memorial Building during construction. The Maxwell House plant to the rear remains in service. The shipyards have disappeared. Courtesy of the William Morgan Collection, University of Florida Libraries.

Right: Figure 88. Early photo of the Police Memorial Building shows features of its rooftop park. Its architect appears in the foreground (in brown jacket, his back to the camera). Courtesy of the William Morgan Collection, University of Florida Libraries.

of engineers and consultants and got to work implementing the design's system of twenty-seven-foot-square concrete "trees." On the eastern side of the building the trees created a four-story atrium that Morgan surrounded with railed landings on each floor. This feature, which offered a view of a long central corridor, allowed interaction between employees and other visitors.

The facility, completed in 1975, occupies two city blocks in downtown Jacksonville and consists of parking, service, and sally ports on the lowest level; police operations and administration on the main levels; and a helicopter pad and rooftop gardens on the upper level. The latter were originally accessible to the public by means of four broad stairways.

Horizontal bands of smooth concrete, separated by highly textured vertical walls of bush-hammered concrete, prevail on both the building's interior and exterior spaces. Skylights, rather than windows, introduce daylight into the secure interior space. The facility was built as Morgan designed it, with shade trees, benches, flower beds, and hedges enhancing publicly accessible rooftop areas. "We selected a tree type that had a small root ball and we were very conscious of that. They represented a heavy load, but their location corresponded exactly to the columns that penetrated the building to the foundation," Morgan explained. These natural trees effectively were extensions of the concrete "trees" below, in the building's interior.

Architects Kevin Roche and John Dinkeloo on the West Coast had previously designed a rooftop garden for the Oakland Museum of Art, in California. It inspired Morgan, who researched the techniques they had employed to support rooftop gardens. "It was not a pie in the sky idea, and I wanted to do something that would enhance the city," he said. "The building was intended to be used by all the citizens of the city, and to invite people to use the stairs and to be in their urban environments, and to be aware of the city as a whole, and to have a place for people to congregate and celebrate the experience of being in the city."

To Morgan, the design allowed for pedestrians to move freely through the downtown hardscape. As he had envisioned the building working, a pedestrian on Jacksonville's Forsyth

Street would be able to ascend to the rooftop terraces and cross by way of platforms, terraces, and stairs to descend on the other side to reach to Bay Street, a block to the south: "The whole idea of moving freely without having chokepoints had magnanimous characteristics, and magnanimity does not scare me at all," Morgan said. "I regard that as an intelligent and highly desirable characteristic of any urban setting."

An important aspect of the project was the need to design for ready access to police vehicles, but Morgan's approach to urban architecture sought to minimize the visible impact of automobiles. His competitors' plans called for building multi-story parking facilities occupying a single city block with a connection from the garage to the administrative offices. In contrast, Morgan carved a wedge of space into the gentle hillside on the northern limits of the building site. The space effectively comprises a semi-underground parking area beneath the mass of the Police Memorial Building floating above. "My plan scrambles all that up and puts the officer and vehicle in one integrated facility," he said. "There is no special structure for vehicles and this extends all over the two-block area."

Many of the building's exterior surfaces, but especially large walls facing the recessed parking facilities, were covered in bush-hammered concrete, a design element often deployed during that period by architects creating structures that fall under the rubric of brutalism.

> The way this exterior was created was that when the wall was cast in concrete it had a series of wood members that are nailed to the forms so that you get this sort of corrugated surface. As soon as the forms are removed, or shortly thereafter as soon as the concrete has set up, laborers are shown the wall and they are given ball peen hammers. They smash the corners one after another. It turns out that the Sheriff's Office supplied the laborers from the jail. Guess what these guys did? Two stories high, two blocks long on the wall down there. In letters seventeen feet high in concrete they spelled out, 'The Sheriff eats shit.'"

Each of the building's original terraces had its own individual characteristics; one is still designated as a helicopter pad. The gardens and terraces were delimited by walls, seating areas, and other architectural devices that highlighted the terrace shapes and positions.

Morgan elaborated on the importance of thoughtful design on the livability of cities:

> The building becomes an anchor at the corner of important streets. That's lost in Jacksonville, as a good example. Our streets are lost. Where the hell is the street? We build these new buildings and these plazas are fragments of would-be plazas projecting out. On this corner there's one treatment; on that corner there's another. On that one there's none. They have nothing to do with each other.

Morgan's concept of the Police Memorial Building as a unifying force for the city's fabric arguably failed in this instance. High-rise construction obliterated the building's relationship with the riverfront. Due to security concerns, ongoing problems from vandalism, and the difficulty of maintaining the rooftop garden, the rooftop park features were soon closed to the public. Many aspects persisted, although most were removed with a recent renovation of the building's roof. Despite Morgan's best efforts at selecting and planting trees that would not interfere with the building's stability, the Jacksonville Sheriff's Office and the building's managers believed the trees compromised the roof's integrity, so the landscaping was removed.

During the fortieth anniversary celebration of the Pyramid Condominium in 2015, one of the residents telephoned William Morgan to congratulate him. He said the building looked like new and was completely occupied. The caller wanted to thank the architect for designing a great building four decades earlier and asked him if he could sign current photographs for the residents. It was a fitting tribute to Morgan's vision and inventive construction methods, which the Pyramid exemplified.

Morgan's design for the building in Ocean City, Maryland, was a response to its oceanfront site. The building's triangular shape and interlocking spaces provide a rising, falling, airy, and

Police Memorial Building
501 E. BAY ST

Facing page: Figure 89. Contemporary view from the river side of the Police Memorial Building. It is connected to the John E. Goode Pre-Trial Detention Facility, to its north. Major changes include removal of rooftop foliage and addition of metal railings surrounding elevated terraces. Photo by Brad Chesivoir.

Left: Figure 90. North entrance to Police Memorial Building. Note alternating bands of bush-hammered and smooth concrete on exterior surfaces. The white fence above the stairs (at left) now prevents access by the public to rooftop terraces. Photo by Brad Chesivoir.

Below: Figure 91. Rooftop fountains and other amenities were ultimately removed from the Police Memorial Building. Courtesy of J. Register Company, Inc.

Facing page: Figure 92. Pyramid Condominium, Ocean City, Maryland. Staggered, receding balconies enhance privacy for this large building. Courtesy of the William Morgan Collection, University of Florida Libraries.

undulating arrangement that Morgan believed echoed the rise and fall of the ocean and the dunes. The unusual shape helped to minimize the dimensions of afternoon shadows cast by the structure. It also contrasts mightily with the parade of rectangular apartment buildings and hotels that populate most of the Ocean City beachfront. Morgan described the vista of the Ocean City beachfront as "stultifying" and complained, "It's a wall of tombstones facing the ocean. Instead of welcoming the beach, the buildings become barriers."

Morgan began seeking commissions from the mid-Atlantic states because of a longtime friend from his undergraduate years at Harvard. Jeremiah O'Leary was a fellow alumnus of Harvard College, a navy veteran, and a fellow product of the Graduate School of Design (in city planning). He and Morgan both served in the Navy ROTC at Harvard College.

After graduation Jerry and his friend and MIT graduate George Marcou formed the planning firm Marcou, O'Leary and Associates in Washington, D.C. Morgan's relationship with O'Leary initially brought him a job for a small research center for Westinghouse, near Annapolis, Maryland. The relationship with Marcou, O'Leary and Associates and the promise of more work in that region led Morgan to establish a Washington office. He appointed Ted Strader, another GSD graduate who had worked previously with Marcou and O'Leary, to head a small office near Dupont Circle as he sought commissions from the mid-Atlantic states.

That was how John and Gail Whaley of Ocean City found Morgan and hired him to design the Pyramid Condominium. The couple wanted to build a large oceanfront apartment house of exceptional design in the rapidly expanding resort city. Morgan spoke with them on the telephone and then invited them to Florida to see his work, including the Florida State Museum in Gainesville, then under construction.

Morgan was impressed with his new clients. "The Whaleys were interested in ideas, and that thrilled me," he said. "It showed an opening of intellect. They had a wonderful gift—that insight into architecture that enabled them to see beyond what you could see. Their visit to the Florida State Museum was confirmation of their interest in using me as an architect."

Facing page: Figure 93. Model of Pyramid Condominium, Ocean City, Maryland. Only the building at left was constructed. Courtesy of the William Morgan Collection, University of Florida Libraries.

The Pyramid expanded upon techniques Morgan employed for the fast-drying, high-strength Gunite concrete, which he had first used at the E.L.K. Oil Company project in 1964 and then in the underground Dunehouses in 1975. As mentioned, it set up quickly and was very strong, but he discovered that applying the experimental construction material to a large-scale, twenty-two-story project presented problems.

Morgan described the unique challenges the Pyramid Condominium project presented and how he overcame them:

> We were having a lot of trouble getting concrete up to the top of this structure. One of the towers as planned was sixteen stories, and the other was twenty-two or something . . . I mean, they were way up there, and you try to take concrete up there and putting it where it belongs in the time you have to put it there—it was of great concern to us. One of the contractors came up with the idea. . . . The fellows were down there making the swimming pool for the condominium complex, and they took the Gunite, and they applied it directly to a sheet of plywood, held the sheet of plywood up, then removed the plywood. It was important to remove the plywood quickly, otherwise it would be impossible to do so. After the brief few moments in which the form is in place, but the Gunite as yet has no surface adhesion, you have to be constantly moving the form.
>
> The cement was setting up so fast that it would hold itself in place. We would just cover this steel rebar as we went along. Somebody would stand behind it vibrating it, just to keep it from getting stuck, and moving that form along. That's a wall! I mean, we were doing some goofy things, and we were succeeding.
>
> These concrete panels held the next floor up. There is nothing normal about that building. Anyway, we built it, and it was very experimental in its use of a moving mold. That's what's so expensive about most concrete construction—the mold. You have to build it in wood, then spray it, then remove the wood. The Pyramid Condominium avoided much of that . . . and that building is there today. It's there to stay.

Right: Figure 94. East-facing view of Pyramid Condominium, Ocean City, Maryland. Note the exterior hallways radiating from the central elevator bank. Photo by Brad Chesivoir.

Facing page: Figure 95. View from the northeast. Note the contrast with the Pyramid's more recent neighbors. The recessed pyramidal shape not only mimics the undulation of the dunes but also minimizes the shadow cast by the building on the beach. Photo by Brad Chesivoir.

In retrospect, Morgan believed that the design was not as dynamic as it could have been. For example, to reduce production costs, the apartments were standardized with interior spaces that Morgan considered relatively unexciting. Still, the units each had views of both the Atlantic Ocean and Assawoman Bay, with outdoor passageways instead of narrow hallways.

Cost savings with the Pyramid enabled Morgan to experiment with technology and to build an entirely unorthodox arrangement of spaces. The project was originally planned to include three buildings of similar design, but oil shocks and economic recession during the 1970s made travel to Maryland's Eastern Shore less attractive, and the project became limited to a single building.

One of Morgan's best known and most complex works is the 1979 U.S. Federal Building and Courthouse in downtown Fort Lauderdale. Pedestrians enter the five-story building by way of a multi-level courtyard with landscaped gardens, water terraces, and seating areas. Morgan was proud of these features, which he considered "scale-giving elements" that made the massive building friendlier. "I think so many courthouses scare me," Morgan recalled. "You walk into it and you think you're not going to get a straight deal. You feel like a convict instead of a free man."

The building consists of thirty-foot cross-shaped concrete trees with concrete branches that form identical ten-foot-square modules. The precursor for this structural arrangement was the tree system that Morgan developed several years earlier for the Police Memorial Building in Jacksonville, which efficiently integrates utility and structural systems.

Balconies, which are carved deeply into the façades, visually enrich the structure's corners. Similarly, projecting and receding floors enliven the building's megalithic mass under the penetrating South Florida sun. When it opened, stairways leading to all five levels made the building entirely accessible to the public. The structure brings an unusual amount of light and air, as well as a sense of being in South Florida, into its offices and into the judges' chambers themselves, all of which were built on balconies. Morgan was pleased with the result.

> You see these windowed vestibules and each of these floors is expressed. As they rise, each floor recedes at the same rate as the one below and the one above. So, as they go up they all recede. You have this sense of recession and progression as you walk through the building. These planes are coming out and going over you, and they're bridges to space. I think it's unexpected, but it works as a building, and that's the important thing.

The link between this progression/regression of spaces and early architecture was not lost on Morgan, who believed that early builders would have been interested in building reverse pyramids, had they had the technology. The Federal Building and Courthouse was completed as Morgan was finishing his first published book—on pre-Columbian architecture of eastern North America.

Architectural historian Jean-François Lejeune noted that the building "pushed the concept of outdoor organization to its limit."

> There are no inner circulations between the various elevators and waiting lobbies to the courtrooms. Those can only be accessed from the various levels of terraces, which are partially protected from sun and rain by recessed sections and are interconnected by a grand pyramidal staircase that once again exposes his fascination with pre-Columbian architecture.[3]

For Morgan it was important that the building contribute to the streetscape of downtown Fort Lauderdale. As with Jacksonville's Police Memorial Building, it offered places for people to rest, relax, and perhaps have lunch—but in the Fort Lauderdale building these were in shady interior spaces rather than open terraces. It also served as an outdoor waiting station with protection from harsh weather. The intersection of Northeast Third Avenue and East Broward Boulevard was a major bus transfer point, and Morgan figured that into his design. "It was very much a building of the city, for the city. It was a place where people could wait for

Century 21
JOHN F. RING
REALTOR

Facing page: Figure 96. Federal Building and Courthouse, Fort Lauderdale, Florida, view from the southwest. Like the Jacksonville police building, this structure combined public amenities with aspects of pre-Columbian architecture and Morgan's "tree" system of design. Courtesy of the William Morgan Collection, University of Florida Libraries.

Left: Figure 97. Federal Building and Courthouse, Fort Lauderdale. Early photo highlights landscaping, seating, and shade in public areas. Courtesy of the William Morgan Collection, University of Florida Libraries. Photo by Robert Lautman.

transportation, wait for people to pick them up or drop them off," he explained. "It became a hub for activities in the city. It didn't have to grow that way. It was built that way."

This was echoed by comments in *Architectural Record*, which declared, "Ft. Lauderdale has a new building that looks *like* it is downtown and not in the middle of a suburban nowhere. More importantly, it sets a direction for future land use that will bring cohesion to that downtown."[4]

Morgan considered the Federal Building and Courthouse one of his proudest achievements, but as of this writing the building is threatened. Judges, politicians, and civic leaders have attacked the building as inadequately sized, moldy, leaky, and lacking basic security standards, and the federal government has been exploring options for replacing it.[5] Civic leaders are also considering public-private partnerships as an alternative method of financing a replacement building.[6]

The design for the 1979 Daniel State Office Building in Jacksonville, Florida, combined several components that Morgan considered important in any responsible urban structure, including public amenities, hidden parking, and preservation of river views for buildings farther inland. It also reflected motifs of early builders in the Americas.

As with the Police Memorial Building in downtown Jacksonville and the Federal Building and Courthouse he had designed for downtown Fort Lauderdale, Morgan envisioned a building that would inject life into its downtown. In particular, he wanted the Daniel State Office Building to increase opportunities for residents of Jacksonville to enjoy their waterfront. "I think that all buildings should contribute something, not just occupy space, but give something back to the city that will make it a richer place," he said. "In this case, multiple platforms overlook the St. Johns River. The platforms created a waterfront park." The four terraces are arranged in a stepwise array, much like a pyramid. Morgan pointed to its use of this *talud-tablero* pattern found in Teotihuacán and other Mesoamerican sites with pyramids. The terraces originally faced an elevated stage, which was protected by a tensile roof designed

Figure 98. Although empty, the fountains remain from the original design. The Fort Lauderdale Federal Building and Courthouse may soon be replaced. Courtesy of Jean-François Lejeune.

Right: Figure 99. Early photograph of the Daniel State Office Building, Jacksonville, Florida. This east-facing view illustrates how the low-rise, stepped design was intended to blend with the adjacent St. Johns River and avoid interfering with views from inland. Several levels of interior parking help to preserve riverfront space, which was squandered by surface lots beyond the building. Courtesy of the William Morgan Collection, University of Florida Libraries.

Facing page: Figure 100. The Daniel Building also served as a riverfront amphitheater, as shown here. Note the tensile structure that protected the stage. These features were eliminated when the building was absorbed into the hotel complex. Courtesy of the William Morgan Collection, University of Florida Libraries.

Facing page: Figure 101. Exterior view of Daniel Building, Jacksonville, Florida, highlighting its quasi-pyramidal shape. Photo was taken from under the tensile roof covering a stage, which has since disappeared. Courtesy of the William Morgan Collection, University of Florida Libraries. Photo by Bob Braun.

Left: Figure 102. Interior view of Daniel Building showing play of light on bush-hammered concrete surfaces. Courtesy of the William Morgan Collection, University of Florida Libraries. Photo by Bob Braun.

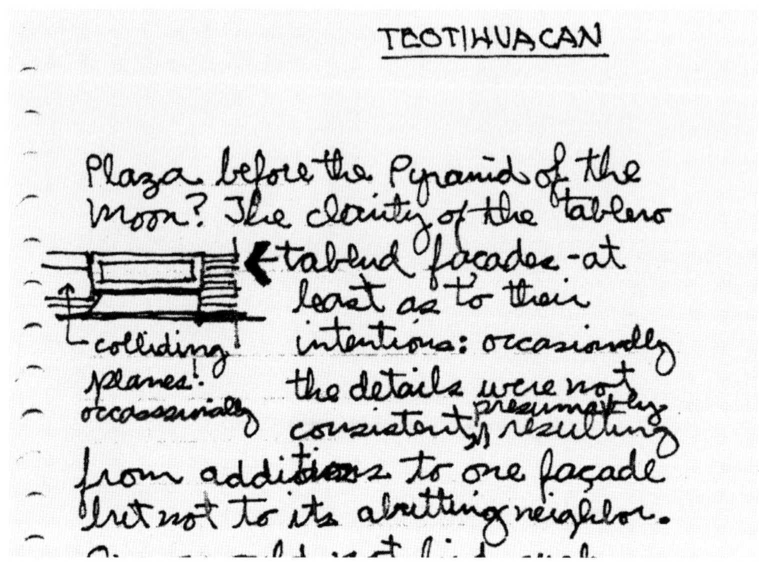
TEOTIHUACAN

Plaza before the Pyramid of the Moon? The clarity of the tablero tablud façades - at least as to their intentions: occasionally the details were not consistent, presumably resulting from additions to one façade but not to its abutting neighbor.

colliding planes! occasionally

Figure 103. Morgan's notes on Mesoamerican building characteristics, some of which are reflected in the design of the Daniel Building and other structures. Courtesy of the William Morgan Collection, University of Florida Libraries.

by Horst Berger. Morgan regarded the terraces as a potent scale-giving element that helped to humanize this government edifice.

Like the Police Memorial Building and the Fort Lauderdale Federal Building and Courthouse, which also was completed in 1979, the Daniel Building includes parking facilities integrated into the structure that avoided the wasted space of exterior stand-alone garages or surface parking lots. The parking facilities are hidden on the lower levels of a rectangular portion of the building, facing the city side of the property. Morgan resisted the impact of automobiles on the urban landscape.

> In this building, in the (Fort Lauderdale) courthouse, in the police building, cars are always on the lower floor and hidden from view—always. It's a matter of respect for the human being, and that's my first priority—not automobiles; human beings. So I get the

cars out of view. We can't afford parking structures and I don't think they (cars) deserve special structures of their own, but we can afford to integrate them into our buildings so we have an entire ground floor directly accessible to the surrounding streets.

Morgan chose the stepped design partly to preserve the river view for existing and future buildings inland from the Daniel Building site. The terraces also avoided the "tombstone" effect along many urban waterfronts that Morgan criticized, such as when he described typical beachfront construction adjacent to the Pyramid Condominium site in Ocean City, Maryland. Morgan envisioned the Daniel Building as a model for a new building profile on Jacksonville's riverfront. He produced drawings for a long-range plan to line the river with a series of similar buildings. Morgan viewed the stepped tiers of the Daniel Building and its low-slung profile as a more sensible approach for development along the St. Johns River, rather than lining it with a wall of high-rise rectangles, which create a barrier to the city's most important feature.

> I made a proposal that the entire waterfront of Jacksonville conform to an imaginary plane that would make the waterfront and the harbor a bowl that would be visible from all around and from the inside. From some distance inshore the high-rise buildings could actually see the riverfront. The way it is now, you can't even see the river because of this monster hotel.[7] I think the greatest focus of Jacksonville should be the river, and I think our attempts at making parks along the river are flimsy compared to the magnificence of the St. Johns River. It should be a celebration of the city in every event. Instead we have this lazy, simple-minded drunk.

The quasi-pyramidal shape avoided a vertical wall facing the river. Its shape also made possible planted areas and rooftop gardens—outdoor spaces where state employees could relax and enjoy a dimension of the office and the city that they otherwise would not have. "Everything in a building should be part of a composition," said Morgan of the relationship between

Figure 104. The Daniel Building is now part of the Hyatt Regency Riverfront hotel. Street access to the central staircase has been blocked. Light fixtures and fencing clutter the building's original appearance. Photo by the author.

his public buildings and the communities they serve. "The composition is a gift to the city and the environment. It should not just grab all that it can and grab all the view and all the access. It should become part of the city. That's what these pyramidal buildings, step terraces, and rooftop gardens all do."

As part of an urban renewal program in the late 1990s, the Daniel Building was given to the developers of a new Adam's Mark Hotel (most recently the Hyatt Regency Jacksonville Riverfront), and it was absorbed into a hotel complex that includes 963 rooms, some of which occupy the former state office building. In the process many of the Daniel Building's most distinctive features, such as its vast use of bush-hammered concrete in the interior, were obscured by more conventional surfaces. Sadly, public access to the riverfront terraces has been severed.

9

Author and Architect

Morgan published the first of his five books on early architecture and earth architecture in 1980: *Prehistoric Architecture in the Eastern United States*. As noted earlier, his interest in the subject grew out of childhood exposure to pueblos and ruins in the American Southwest. The book's preface liberally acknowledges the influence of Ripley Bullen at the University of Florida, who hired Morgan to develop its Florida State Museum. Bullen directed the architect to numerous sites in the Southeast and referred him to other scholars. Morgan also benefited from research provided by Arthur Drexler, Ludwig Glaeser, and the Museum of Modern Art.

The book provides what Morgan identified as the first "comprehensive publication for interested laymen, students, and architects" on early architecture in Eastern North America.[1] It examines eighty-two early sites (from more than four hundred identified) and is organized by historical periods, beginning in 2200 BCE and continuing to about 1500. It generally follows a format used in a 1973 book Morgan had that explored pre-Columbian architecture in Mesoamerica.[2]

His own book about the eastern United States was illustrated with exquisite drawings by two architects on Morgan's staff, William Ebert and Thomas McCrary. When business slowed down at the architectural practice, Morgan would put his architects to work on his books rather than laying them off. He also would take advantage of slack periods to research

Figure 105. Mid-1970s photograph at Copán, Honduras, of Morgan and family. *Left to right*: Newt, Dylan, Bunny, and William. From the Morgan family.

archaeological subjects—both in the office and in the field. Between 1980 and 1994 he authored three more books on ancient architecture, covering the American Southwest (and parts of Mexico), Micronesia, and eastern North America.

As Morgan became more immersed in his research, his architectural designs continued to explore concepts he identified in ancient buildings and spaces. He also deployed other ideas in architecture, partly out of the challenge but also because the public in his hometown increasingly rejected his bold visions for public architecture. Morgan succeeded in attracting large commissions outside Jacksonville, including Neiman Marcus and Bloomingdale's department stores in South Florida, but his local work increasingly was residential architecture, which—due to the practical limitations of a building site or client preferences—less frequently involved the influences of earth architecture or early architecture and instead explored other concepts.

Morgan returned to the truncated pyramid, however, with his design for the Oceanfront Townhouses in Atlantic Beach, completed in 1982. High school friend and client George Goodloe and Morgan together invested in an expanse of property that extended from the beachfront on 19th Street in Atlantic Beach west to Seminole Road. The Goodloes planned to occupy the main unit in the center. The Morgans would take possession of one of the adjacent units, with the third serving as a rental. Later the architect traded his unit for the large parcel occupying the entire north side of 19th Street, between Beach Avenue and Seminole Road, the "back 40," as he referred to it. Morgan subsequently designed and developed five houses along that block. (A sixth lot remains undeveloped as of this writing.)

For the Oceanfront Townhouses Morgan designed a truncated pyramid structure, which was set into a high dune, preserving an ocean view for neighbors farther inshore. Each unit in the triplex would have an oceanfront view, as would its neighbors to the west. Morgan had followed this principle in his urban riverfront projects in downtown Jacksonville, in the Daniel State Office Building, and the Police Memorial Building, which sought to protect the views of existing and future inland structures.

The low-sloping roof on the truncated pyramid not only preserved ocean views for neighbors; it also invoked design themes from early builders. "A familiar architectural technique of mine is to use early shapes in modern buildings," Morgan observed. "The sand dunes are very pliable and the contours of the sand dunes lend themselves to the truncated pyramid shape employed with this structure. You couldn't see the beach if you had a rectangular wall blocking the way."

As with Morgan's own residence and the adjacent Dunehouses, the lot is higher inshore than at the beachfront, resulting in a tilted site. The building's truncated pyramidal shape corresponds to the uses of the three attached dwellings. Two three-bedroom units with sloping roofs flank a central three-bedroom unit. Each unit includes its own private garden, private entrances, and carports that are built into the mass of the truncated pyramid.

Entering the Naval Submarine Base in Kings Bay, Georgia, one sees a retention pond, which provides a reflection of adjacent twin pyramidal structures—Fluckey Hall. In pre-Columbian times buildings in the Southeast had been composed of lineal berms and truncated pyramids. The architect believed these forms had meaning appropriate to the Trident submarine base commander and his support staff.

This complex, finished in 1987, houses the multiple functions of a nuclear submarine base in two distinct components. As conceived, the organizational structure of the facility is reflected in its architecture. A truncated pyramid housing the admiral's headquarters hovers over a second truncated pyramid containing administrative areas. Morgan thought the relationship of the pyramids would remind visitors and workers of the organizational structure of the headquarters. The architect was enthusiastic about the numerous archaeological sites nearby and suspected that pre-Columbian builders on those sites used similar organizational devices in their building designs to represent the power dynamics of their culture, as is evidenced in other early sites in North America and Mesoamerica.

An ivy-covered earthen berm houses the first floors of both pyramids. In front of the administration building's entrance is an open-air plaza focused on a flagpole. As many of the functions within the building are highly sensitive, the building was not designed to be particularly open, apart from the main entrance, which was carved into the ivy-covered, east-facing berm.

Architect William Ebert worked on the project for Morgan and thought the Kings Bay facility was a perfect application for an earthen-berm structure.

Facing page: Figure 106. View from the beach of the Oceanfront Townhouses, Atlantic Beach, Florida. The low-slung truncated pyramid blended into the dune and preserved the view of the beach from inland properties owned by Morgan. Locals frequently refer to the building as the "spaceship." Photo by Brad Chesivoir.

Facing page: Figure 107. Image facing northwest showing detail of main entrance to Fluckey Hall. The brick façade harmonizes with much of the traditional architecture found elsewhere on the base. Photo by Brad Chesivoir.

> I thought that was a really innovative building in that if you're an architect who wants to do berm structures, you might want to do them on everything. But in some places it doesn't make sense. There it made perfect sense. One of the buildings was the headquarters building and the other was the subgroup headquarters for the head of the Atlantic group of submarines. Underneath in the bermed area of the subgroup area was all the communications equipment. The earth and RF (radio frequency) shielding helped to make it secure.

A subsequent residential project provided Morgan an opportunity to explore design principles of Florida's vernacular architecture. Surfing enthusiast George Grandy had specific requirements when he hired Morgan to design a home for him on the western side of an ancient dune in Atlantic Beach. Grandy wanted a thirty-five-foot-high observation deck (as high as the building code permitted) so that he could monitor surf conditions along Atlantic Beach. He also required wide porches for entertaining, a metal roof for added storm protection, two equal but separate bedrooms for his two teenage daughters, and a two-car garage accessible from the west.

Morgan designed a house that borrowed characteristics of traditional southeastern U.S. houses. Grandy liked the conventions of southern vernacular architecture, and he was not inclined toward Morgan's modernist visions, and Morgan complied. The residence, completed in 1990, was built from wood frame with wood siding and a first floor lifted above grade by cylindrical concrete piers. It featured a metal roof of the kind commonly seen in the countryside of the American Southeast.

As with many of his projects in Atlantic Beach, Morgan respected the landscape upon which he built. He laid out the Grandy Residence over the western edge of the same ancient dune that forms the basis for Morgan's four oceanfront designs. Rather than flattening the dune prior to construction, his design preserved it with a judicious use of concrete piers that elevate portions of the house and enable it to hover above the dune's steep western slope.

Left: Figure 108. Model of Naval Submarine Base, Kings Bay, Georgia. Morgan was particularly aware of the hierarchical relationship of structures and use of ceremonial spaces, particularly in governmental settings. Courtesy of the William Morgan Collection, University of Florida Libraries.

Above: Figure 109. Earthen berms and pyramids feature prominently in the construction, which was designed to reflect early earthen architecture in the region. Photo by Brad Chesivoir.

The building forms a U-shape around a central area, which surrounded an existing bay tree. The tree later died and was replaced by palms, ferns, and other plants. The central U-shaped courtyard divides the house between more private spaces to the west and areas for entertaining that face the ocean to the east. A central passageway connects the two wings and also houses the kitchen. The large master bedroom on the upper level faces the ocean and includes a spiral staircase to a small balcony with a clear view of the Atlantic.

As Grandy requested, vehicular access to the property is from the west, in part to avoid interference with the bold appearance of the residence's eastern façade. Uncharacteristic of Morgan's other Atlantic Beach designs, the Grandy Residence includes a two-car garage, discreetly built into the dune, rather than a carport.

The Grandys also purchased a second fifty-foot-wide lot south of the main one. They intended to leave that lot in a natural state, while reserving it for future development. The residence's next owners, whom Morgan characterized as having "an exceptional exposure to modern architecture and design," elected to build a lap pool, entertainment area, and small pavilion on a portion of that unimproved lot. Morgan had feared that enhancements to the south would compete with the original structure, and he convinced the new residents to hire a landscape architect to create a design for the southern lot. After its completion, Morgan was pleased with the result.

During this period, beginning in 1983, Morgan researched and finalized his second book, *Prehistoric Architecture in Micronesia.* Inspiration for the work began with his navy experiences in the South Pacific in the early 1950s. He remained intrigued with what he had seen in Guam and other islands, and his interest was reignited after reading about early Micronesian architecture in a National Geographic Society publication.

As with his previous work on early building in eastern North America, this book is organized around geographical groupings and includes intricate drawings by members of his architectural staff. Unlike the previous work, *Prehistoric Architecture in Micronesia* includes

Right: Figure 110. The architect poses before the eastern side of the newly completed Grandy Residence, Atlantic Beach, Florida. From the Morgan family.

Facing page: Figure 111. Grandy Residence elevation. As originally conceived, the plan preserved and celebrated a large tree, which was enveloped by the U-shaped design. Courtesy of the William Morgan Collection, University of Florida Libraries.

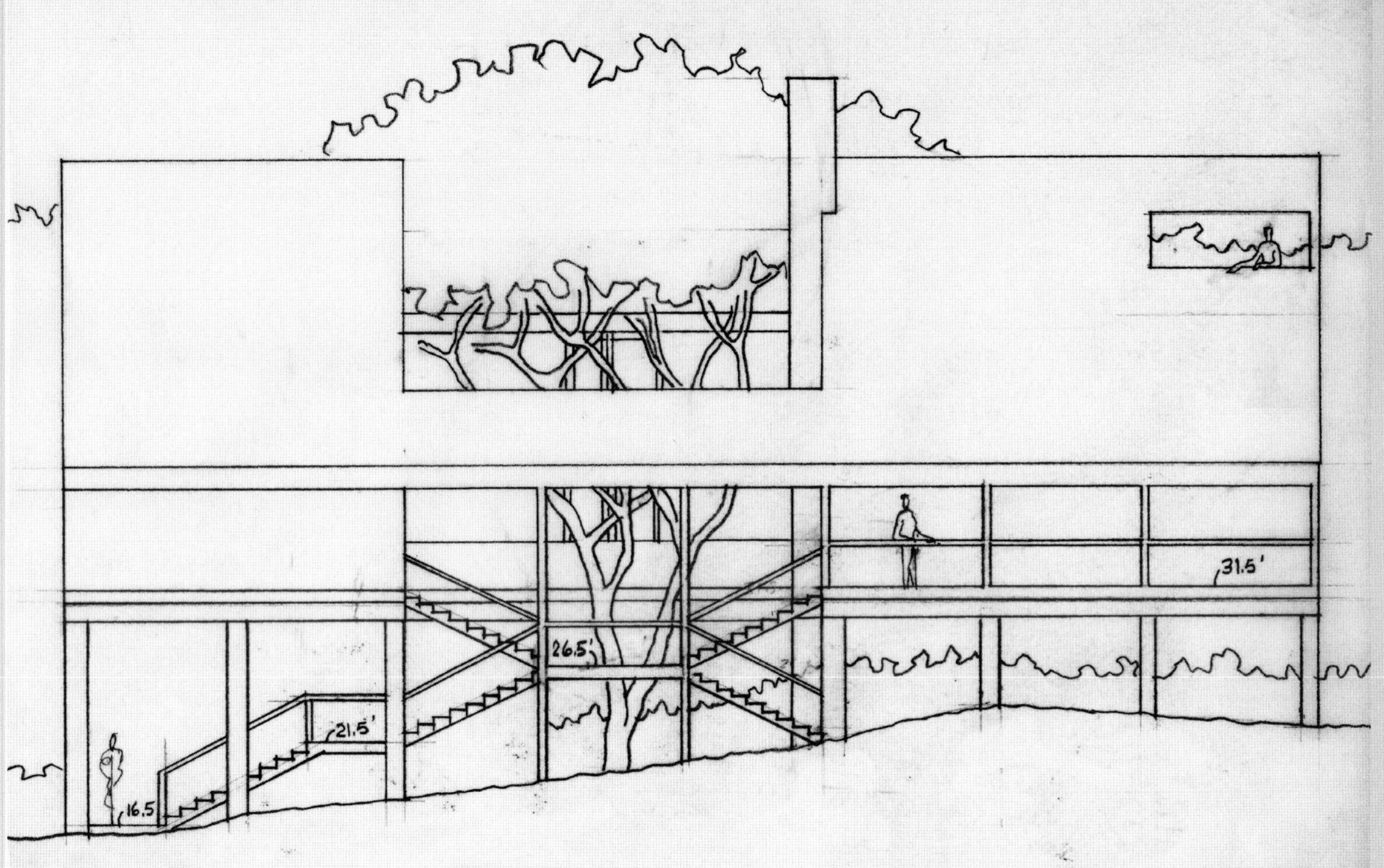

SOUTH ELEVATION
1/8"=1'-0"

GRANDY RESIDENCE SCHEMATICS
WM. MORGAN ARCHTS. 10 DEC. '88

Right: Figure 112. Grandy Residence interior, facing east. The second-floor living room of the Grandy Residence is surrounded by a covered porch. Photo by Brad Chesivoir.

Facing page: Figure 113. Contemporary photo of the Grandy Residence reveals a lap pool and revised landscaping. The architect approved. Photo by Brad Chesivoir.

original photography by his son Newton Morgan shot during trips to Pohnpei, Kosrae, Yap, Palau, the Mariana Islands, and the Hawaiian Islands.

For a new U.S. Embassy in Khartoum, Sudan, the Department of State was concerned with security. A suicide bomber had attacked and destroyed much of the Beirut Embassy only a few years earlier. In the late 1980s and early part of the next decade, Morgan's firm was busy with two designs for the embassy that were never realized.

Morgan visited the site on the White Nile three times over a period of as many years and spent many hours learning about the state of the art of architecture in Sudan. For inspiration

he traveled north to visit southern Nubia and the ruins of the once great city of Musawwarat es-Sufra.

"I was intrigued by the ancient architecture that predated Christian, Muslim, and British influences," he recalled. Morgan was drawn to the truncated pyramids that line the eastern edge of the city. He proposed to shape the embassy building into the form of an inverted pyramid supported by four symmetrical pylons, each several stories high. As he saw it, the architecture would recall Sudan's past accomplishments in modern terms. However, Morgan's inverted pyramid design was scrapped, and the firm supplied a more conventional design for a two-story edifice with two courtyards. In the meantime, U.S. relations with emerging African nations deteriorated, and interest in a new embassy for Sudan was withdrawn. Still, Morgan considered the unbuilt project a lifesaver for the firm, because it provided income during an otherwise quiet period.

When there was no business, Morgan kept busy with his archaeological research. His third book, *Ancient Architecture of the Southwest,* published in 1994, resulted from research and field visits during the latter part of the 1980s and early 1990s and was funded by a grant from the National Endowment for the Arts. As with his *Prehistoric Architecture in the Eastern United States*, this work is organized chronologically and then geographically. It includes detailed drawings executed by his architectural staff. Despite the title, the book includes living Zuni, Hopi, and Rio Grande pueblos and some ancient sites in Mexico that are linked to the Mogollon culture. The UNESCO World Heritage Site Paquimé in Casas Grandes, Chihuahua, Mexico, is featured on the book's dust jacket.

Later in the 1990s Jacksonville-based Reynolds, Smith and Hills—Morgan's first employers as a GSD graduate—hired Morgan as a design consultant for a project to build a new U.S. Courthouse in Tallahassee. The building was completed in 2000, after many years of delay. Its design, to a large extent, reflects the relatively conservative preferences of the judges. Increased security concerns, following bombing of Oklahoma City's Murrah Building in 1995, prevented the public accessibility that was a key feature of Morgan's Fort Lauderdale federal

Above: Figure 114. The family's 1984 trip to Micronesia demanded resourcefulness. Here William Morgan opens a coconut. From the Morgan family.

Right: Figure 115. William and Dylan Morgan at the wall tomb of Inol, a truncated pyramid structure in eastern Micronesia. From the Morgan family.

UNITED STATES COURTHOUSE
UNITED STATES COURTHOUSE

courthouse project, completed twenty-one years earlier. He interviewed the judges, and their cooperation was an important factor in the design and furnishings of the Tallahassee courthouse—inside and outside. Morgan shared how these conversations with the tradition-loving judges affected his design: "After interviewing the judges individually, I formed the opinion that they probably would be happy with the Campidoglio in Renaissance Rome," he said. This would be Morgan's last commission for a large public building.

With a scaled-down practice, Morgan was able to devote more time to research and also to teaching. He lectured at Jacksonville University, the Savannah College of Art and Design, and Florida A&M University. He also taught classes on pre-Columbian North American archaeology at Jacksonville University and the University of North Florida. In 1998 he was appointed to the Beinecke-Reeves Chair in Architectural Preservation at the University of Florida. During the next two years Morgan lectured at the university's Vicenza Institute of Architecture in Italy and conducted walking tours for architectural students in that country and in Croatia.

Morgan also continued his research in archaeology and earth architecture. *Precolumbian Architecture in Eastern North America*, published in 1999, updated and expanded his original work on the subject. The revised edition reproduced the earlier book's intricate drawings. Its retail price was minimized by providing online access to color plates.

Amid this activity Morgan created a powerful design for the beachfront lot he owned to the north of his own house. The 2002 Dylan Morgan House became part of an integral design that included his own residence and the adjacent Dunehouses. "There is a value that we as architects cannot bring into being. Nature has this great power to reshape the shoreline with a sweep of the arm. It's worth celebrating and I think that's what these houses do," Morgan later said, referring to the grouping of three idiosyncratic dwellings.

Morgan candidly acknowledged the influence of Le Corbusier's Villa Baizeau, in Carthage, Tunisia, with the use of pilotis and interlocking one-story and two-story spaces to provide air circulation in the Dylan Morgan House as well as cantilevered surfaces to provide shade.

Facing page: Figure 116. U.S. Courthouse, Tallahassee, Florida. View facing east. The conservative nature of the building largely reflects heavy involvement by its judges in the building's design. Photo by Charles Badland.

Above: Figure 117. Morgan taught at the University of Florida's Vicenza Institute of Architecture campus in Italy and led architectural tours in Europe for students and faculty. From the Morgan family.

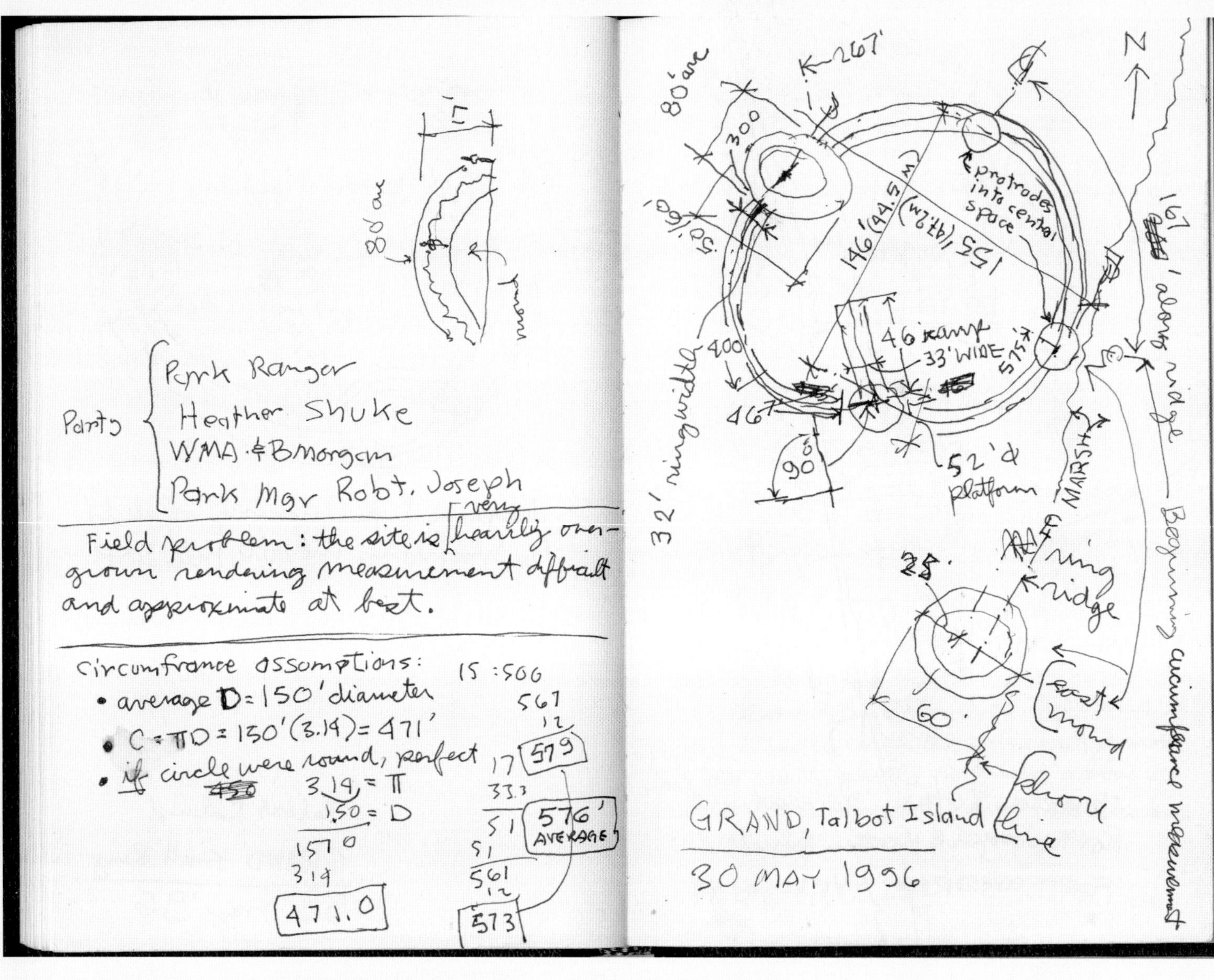

80' arc
mound
Party
Park Ranger
Heather Shuke
WMA & B Morgan
Parks Mgr Robt. Joseph
Field problem: the site is very heavily overgrown rendering measurement difficult and approximate at best.
circumfrance assomptions:
• average D = 150' diameter
• C = πD = 150'(3.14) = 471'
• if circle were round, perfect
3.14 = π
150 = D
471.0
579
576' AVERAGE
573
267'
80' arc
300
protrudes into central space
146' (44.5 m)
155' (47.2 m)
46' ramp
33' WIDE
400
467'
90°
52' d platform
32' ring width
MARSH
167' along ridge
Beginning circumference measurement
ring ridge
25'
60'
east mound
shore line
N
GRAND, Talbot Island
30 MAY 1996

Facing page: Figure 118. Example of Morgan's field notes on earth architecture. In this case he was estimating the original size of an earthen mound near Jacksonville, Florida. Courtesy of the William Morgan Collection, University of Florida Libraries.

Left: Figure 119. Dylan Morgan House from beach side with view of William Morgan Residence to the south. Cantilevered decks maximize beach vistas while also providing shade. Courtesy of the William Morgan Collection, University of Florida Libraries.

Right: Figure 120. Interior of Dylan Morgan House. Large windows maximize views of the Atlantic Ocean. Courtesy of the William Morgan Collection, University of Florida Libraries.

Facing page: Figure 121. Viewed from the beach, left to right, are the Dunehouses, William Morgan House, and Dylan Morgan House. Although remodeling of the Dunehouses diminished their simplicity, the thoughtful grouping of these different structures remains striking. Photo by Brad Chesivoir.

Setback requirements restricted the building's width to thirty-five feet and its maximum height to thirty-five feet, factors that contributed to its verticality. Two carports are accessible to the west by way of Beach Avenue, which follows the shoreline along the crest of the dune. Located between the carports, the main entry leads past a central stairway to the kitchen, dining room, two-story living room, and balcony—all facing the Atlantic Ocean.

The low-ceiling entry hall expands vertically into a two-story-high living room, one of the architect's favorite spatial sequences, which is replicated in many of his designs, including his own residence. A wood-burning fireplace forms the centerpiece of the living room along its north wall. The stairs on the west wall lead up to the east-facing master bedroom suite and to the west-facing children's bedrooms and baths. The lowest level of the residence opens onto the beachfront, with storage space for surfboards and beach paraphernalia located under the house.

Dylan Morgan took pride in the house's original bright orange color, noting that it was one of the few houses his father had designed that were anything but white. Children passing by on bicycles would refer to his residence as the "Cheese House" (and to the subterranean Dunehouses next door as the "Cookie-Monster House").

10

More Recent Projects

One of William Morgan's most recent projects, completed in 2006, is a 5,900-square-foot rectangular beach house designed as a weekend retreat for Georgia real estate developer Francis Lott and his wife, Diane, on Amelia Island, which is located on the northeastern tip of Florida's Atlantic coast.[1]

To begin the design process, Morgan visited his clients in their home in Douglas, Georgia—a community about a two-hour drive from the site—to understand how they lived. The couple's permanent home was a contemporary single-story, wood-framed structure designed by architect Blake Ellis of Valdosta, Georgia. Francis Lott himself earned a degree in architecture from the Georgia Institute of Technology. Although he never practiced as an architect, his vision had a decided impact on Morgan's design. "I aspired for a home far better than I could design for myself. It was just too important," Francis Lott recalled. "So I decided to hire an architect who was the best in the business for the style of house I wanted. That was William Morgan—best decision I've ever made."

The spacious beach house was designed to accommodate simultaneously the Lotts, members of their family, and guests: "The house was set up so at least two families could occupy it at the same time and function more or less independently," Morgan noted. The site is a hundred-foot-wide beachfront lot in a single-family neighborhood of detached vacation houses.

SEALOFT

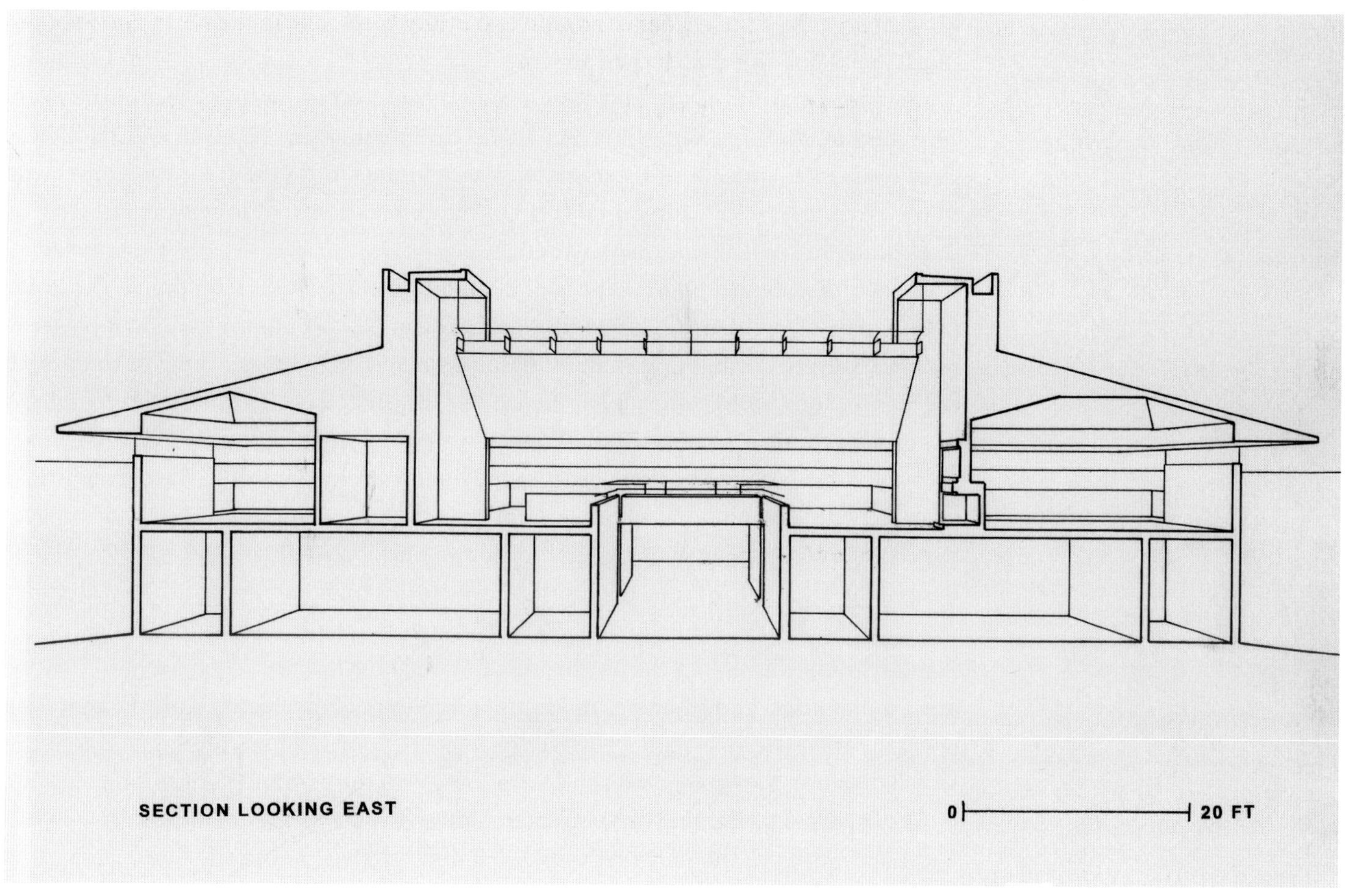

Facing page: Figure 122. Lott Residence, Amelia Island, Florida. View from west. Photo by Walter Elliott.

Above: Figure 123. Lott Residence section. A two-story foyer and open second-floor living/dining/kitchen areas dominate the design. Courtesy of the William Morgan Collection, University of Florida Libraries.

Facing page: Figure 124. Beachside pool area. Photo by Walter Elliott.

Morgan organized the residence around two utility cores, one to the north and another to the south, separated by a landscaped atrium.

Morgan's imprint on the Lott Residence was somewhat limited because the clients had very specific ideas for their home, but he did explore new directions in natural lighting on a large residential scale. "We discussed what was important to them for the house, what they wanted to emphasize," Morgan said. "I got the impression that they were conservative and that I shouldn't pull any nonsense stunts."

Morgan decided to build a two-story building because that would give the Lotts twice the number of rooms with exposures to the ocean. "The building was on a palatial scale," recalled Morgan. Bringing in natural light presented a challenge. "One of the problems of very large rooms anywhere, but particularly by the oceanfront, is there is very bright lighting in perimeter rooms and relative darkness toward the center," Morgan explained. "The larger the room, the darker the center, because the light source is far away." Morgan addressed this problem with a continuous forty-two-foot skylight illuminating the upper floor spaces from the ceiling ridges and by uniting the rooms into one continuous space. Atypical of a Morgan design, the entrance foyer to the house is two stories high and embellished with four triple-stem Christmas palms in copper planters. The main rooms in the residence all face the ocean. Hallways radiate from the balcony overlooking the first-floor courtyard space. "Private living areas to the north and south are modest," Morgan said. "In keeping with the owner's preferences, activities were oriented toward the second-floor kitchen, dining, and living rooms, which overlook the ocean, pool, and terrace areas to the east and the central courtyard."

The backyard swimming pool is centered on an atrium with sunbathing areas to the south and picnic areas to the north. A boardwalk and walkway led to the beach along the north property line. Existing sand dunes were carefully protected, consistent with Morgan's usual policy of preserving the topography and vegetation of building sites.

After signing the design agreement, the clients were impressed that Morgan had prepared a detailed schedule for completion of the various drawings required and a model of the

house. "I had no expectation that any architect—let alone such a creative one—would be so organized," Francis Lott recalled.

This is one of Morgan's larger residential designs, and some of its characteristics deviate from his normal practice. The large scale of the building and its rooms required several adaptations. Morgan remembered the client requesting the two-story foyer and adjacent double staircases. The two garages are also atypical of Morgan's designs; he generally substituted carports for garages, which he regarded as inconvenient because they must be opened and shut when parking. These requirements, as well as demands of a particularly active client, led to a structure that is large, yet one that Morgan managed to make both intimate and livable.

"The result is a house that is better than anything I could have dreamed of having," Francis Lott recalled in 2016. "I marvel every time I walk in the front door. It's still as thrilling today as it was when we first moved in. My wife and I fully recognize we are very fortunate and will be ever indebted to Mr. Morgan for his vision."

Morgan's fifty years studying earth architecture culminated with publication of *Earth Architecture: From Ancient to Modern* in 2008. The book considers fifty-four examples of nine varieties of earth architecture from around the world and reflects Morgan's research during his Wheelwright year and for the four volumes he previously authored. Unlike the previous volumes and unlike the unpublished draft, *Earth Architecture* is primarily illustrated with photographs, although a few drawings from North American sites are reproduced from his previous books.

Morgan's introduction to *Earth Architecture: From Ancient to Modern* speaks to the evolution of his own approach to architecture and the environment.

> During the 50 years or so since I began this study, the way that I think about architecture and the environment seems to have shifted. During the 1950s buildings appeared to exist independently from their sites; structures could be reoriented or relocated largely at will. Frank Lloyd Wright's works respected nature without reservation, but seemingly at a

Facing page: Figure 125. Interior view across living room and atrium, which is planted with large palms. A long skylight illuminates this large space. Photo by Walter Elliott.

Facing page: Figure 126. Quelch-Gendzier Residence, St. Augustine, Florida, view looking north. Morgan described the clients' preferences in architecture as "straightforward and clear-headed." Image courtesy of Antony Rieck.

> distance, and Le Corbusier elevated his structures on stilts so that they safely maintained their detachment from nature. The conception of architecture as a relocatable object in the landscape may have its origin at least in part in our classical Greco-Roman tradition. Gradually my interests have shifted from detachable architecture to structures more closely integrated with their environments.[2]

With some exceptions, one can see that in William Morgan's work. As his career progressed, his designs generally became more sensitive to nature, to place, to location, to history. Even a dwelling as resolutely modernist as the Dylan Morgan House was consciously integrated into the steep gradient of the dune, and doing so harmonizes with the adjacent and much different William Morgan Residence and the Dunehouses.

Morgan's last completed design is a 2009 two-story residence facing a large saltwater marsh in a beach community north of St. Augustine, Florida. The Quelch-Gendzier Residence is more typical of early modernist convention, with unadorned white surfaces interspersed with horizontal bands. Design elements noticeably emerge and recede, as with some of Morgan's earlier work and that of other well-known modernists, such as Le Corbusier and Sert.

The house was designed for a pair of veterinarians with a particular fondness for swimming and for their pets. Its lower floor consists of a two-bay carport that is open to the south. Morgan had a dilemma in siting the house because a neighboring house to the east was built close to the property line and blocked a direct orientation of the Quelch-Gendzier Residence toward the horizon and the Atlantic Ocean. Instead, Morgan created a more oblique orientation to the ocean by facing the home to the northeast rather than directly to the east. The result is a living space with spectacular views of protected marshland, the Tolomato River to the west, and a small slice of the Atlantic visible to the east—and a minimal awareness of neighboring houses.

Two bedrooms on the lower floor and the small foyer at the base of the stairs lead up to two additional levels with a pleasant view of a nature preserve.

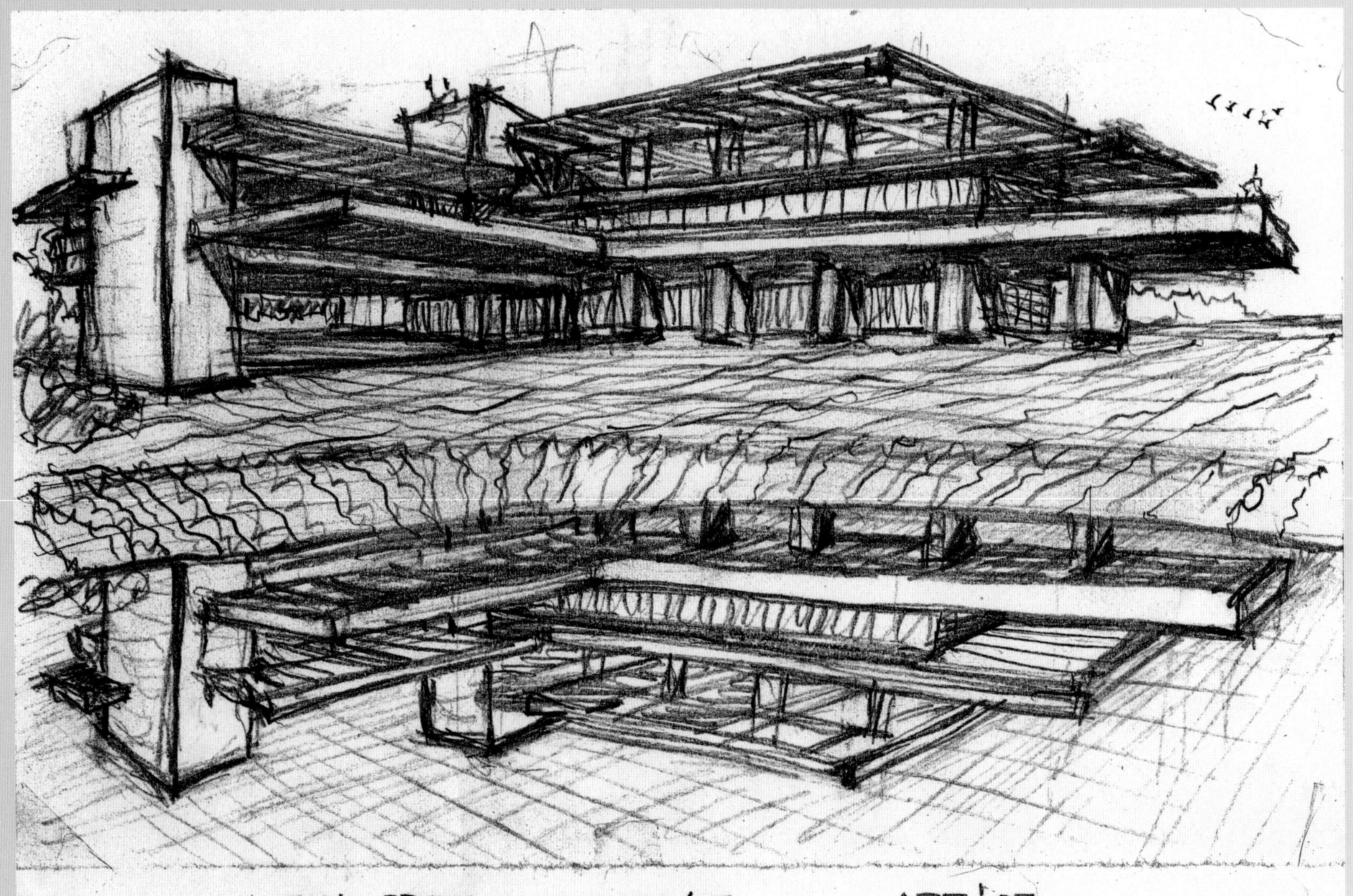
VIEW FROM NORTHEAST
APR '05

Facing page: Figure 127. Quelch-Gendzier Residence, St. Augustine, Florida. The pre-construction drawing depicts the north (marsh) side of the house and its reflection in a small pond. Courtesy of Virginia Quelch.

Left: Figure 128. View of rear, looking toward the southwest. The second floor of the 2,616-square-foot house includes a 40-foot lap pool as well as the living room, dining room, and kitchen. Image courtesy of Antony Rieck.

The building was constructed of reinforced concrete block, consistent with demands of its proximity to the ocean and code requirements, particularly for wind. Given the owners' interest in swimming, Morgan included a narrow lap pool on the second floor, which serves as a central organizational feature for the dwelling.

The architect's clients were delighted with the design process and the result. Mark Gendzier recalled:

> We were searching for an architect for a very long time. My wife and I knew we wanted to build a modern home. We met with one architect who said, "I always wanted to build a tidewater cottage." My heart just sank, and I thought, "Here's another wasted hour." But the architect said, "There's an architect in Atlantic Beach. I don't know if he's still living. He's older. Let me see about introducing you." We had lunch with Bunny and William. He visited our home and wanted to see how we lived. We visited the piece of property. He invited us up to Atlantic Beach to his home. We went up and he brought out a series of pictures he had drawn and views of the home he had designed. My wife and I were blown away. It was just everything we had asked for in a house.

The two veterinarians were impressed by Morgan's ability to formulate a comprehensive design. "I never knew anyone who could X-ray a house with his eyes," Gendzier recalled. The couple made few demands on Morgan. "He had a vision that was very well formed and striking." There was, however, one alteration in the design that they requested. The original design width of the second-floor lap pool was too narrow for Mark Gendzier to swim breaststroke, his favorite. It was modified to accommodate that.

During the construction phase Morgan was weakened by the illness that ultimately felled him in 2016. The contractor built temporary ramps to enable the architect to see his last design nearing completion.

Facing page: Figure 129. Stock photo shot at Quelch-Gendzier Residence. Photo ©iStockphoto.com/Susan Chiang.

Left: Figure 130. William Morgan inspects plans for the Quelch-Gendzier Residence, then under construction. *Left to right*: contractor Edward Main, Virginia Quelch, William Morgan. Courtesy of Virginia Quelch.

Below: Figure 131. William Morgan peering over protected wetland during a visit to the Quelch-Gendzier Residence, then under construction, July 2008. Courtesy of Virginia Quelch.

Morgan was pleased with the Quelch-Gendzier Residence and how he incorporated his design principles into a simple and functionally elegant home for his clients. He said of the structure:

> The building is what it is, and it says so. It does not attempt to be anything more or anything less than it is. By not attempting to be anything more, it says something more. It is well proportioned, beautifully composed, thoughtfully assembled, with materials appropriately selected and expressed. So all together the building becomes a work of art, which is effectively the soul of architecture.

11

Final Thoughts

Morgan's professional career effectively ended with this simple, elegant, and honest expression in the Quelch-Gendzier Residence. Morgan's illness continued to weaken him. He worked in his downtown Jacksonville office until 2008. Later that year he underwent surgery for cancer, after which it was estimated that he had six months more to live, at most.

But Morgan was a fighter. He beat the odds and stretched his life another eight years, and he never gave up hope. During his long fight with cancer and related diseases, the architect designed a new house, equipped with an elevator, for the next stage of his life, although construction never began. He died on January 18, 2016.

In the architectural community, nationally and internationally, Morgan is recognized as one of Florida's most important architects. His body of work has been documented in dozens of articles in the world's leading architectural journals. It continues to attract the attention of architectural historians and television producers, who regularly create features on his 1975 Dunehouses in Atlantic Beach. The University of Florida recognized his contributions by conferring on Morgan an honorary doctorate in 2012, and its School of Architecture bestowed on him a Lifetime Achievement Award in 2013.

William Morgan distinguished himself as an exceptional architect and arguably one of the most important creative forces to emerge from northeast Florida in the twentieth century.

Figure 132. Morgan's design for his next residence at 1942 Beach Avenue, Atlantic Beach. View looking west shows balconies with views over the Dunehouses to the Atlantic Ocean. Courtesy of the William Morgan Collection, University of Florida Libraries.

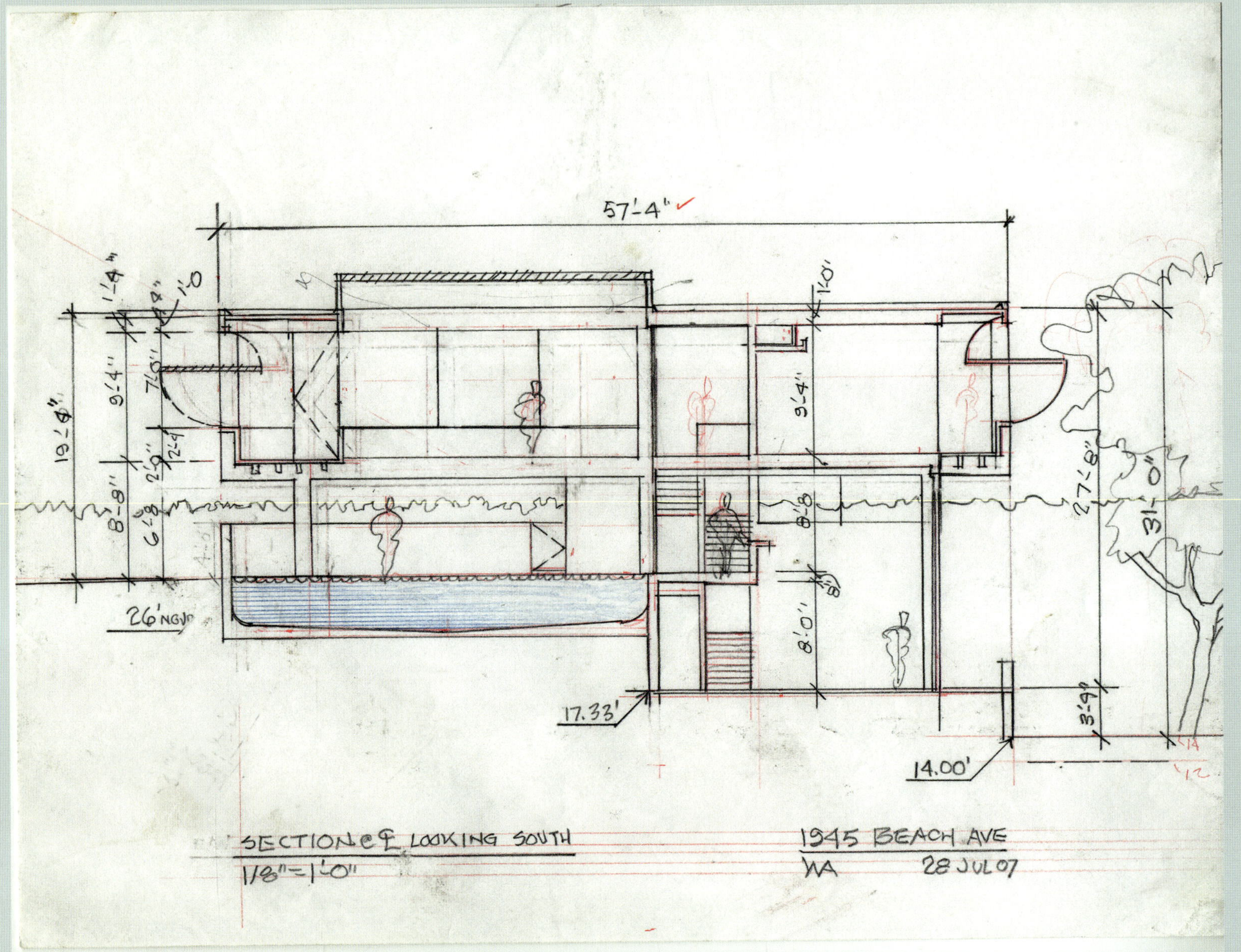
57'-4"
1'-4"
1'-0
9'-4"
7'-0"
19'-4"
2'-0"
8'-8"
6'-8"
26' NGVD
9'-4"
1'-0"
8'-8"
8'-0"
27'-8"
31'-0"
3'-9"
17.33'
14.00'
SECTION @ ℄ LOOKING SOUTH
1/8" = 1'-0"
1945 BEACH AVE
WA
28 JUL 07

His genius can be characterized by several aspects that evolved over his lifetime and over his career.

Morgan took a modernist architectural language that rejected history and infused it with the vocabulary of American prehistory. Educated at Harvard's GSD in the 1950s, Morgan studied there at a time when the school remained a hotbed of Bauhaus-inspired modernists. Although the GSD had reduced the role of history in its curriculum during the Gropius period, by the time Morgan arrived history had been largely restored in the school's architectural curriculum. He embraced it as a student and throughout his practice, including elements of early buildings and landscapes that seldom found more than superficial expression in modern architecture.

The result was an architecture that softened aspects of modernism's buildings for the "machine age" with elements of ancient architecture that subtly and innovatively speak to the history of a place and the historical relationships that exist between buildings and places. But Morgan was not superficially affixing historical design cues, as postmodernists would do. As his career unfolded, he increasingly believed there was much to learn from early architects' responses to building sites, to weather, and to nature. Morgan's most ambitious designs incorporating early motifs were principally for large governmental or educational facilities. In some cases, as with Fluckey Hall at the Naval Submarine Base in Kings Bay, Georgia, the result is respected, admired, and well maintained. The Federal Building and Courthouse in Fort Lauderdale appears to be less fortunate, although the building does have some supporters who argue for preserving and repurposing it.

Introducing ideas of early architects generally had several benefits. It connected modern buildings and places with the past, and this happened in rapidly developing, auto-centric places like Ocean City, Maryland, and in Florida, where the past is typically invisible. Morgan was aware of the spatial arrangements in early landscapes like Kolomoki Mound, near Blakely, Georgia, and Cahokia, near St. Louis, and what they suggested about their builders' social, economic, and political systems. He identified these relationships in early structures

Facing page: Figure 133. Section drawn by Morgan for 1942 Beach Avenue. The design includes an elevator and a lap pool. Adjacent to the Grandy House and across from the Dunehouses, the design accommodates the steep incline of the western side of an ancient dune. The address on the image incorrectly corresponds to his nearby house, which was completed in 1972. Courtesy of the William Morgan Collection, University of Florida Libraries.

and cultures and deployed them in his designs to underline institutional relationships and to render buildings supporting the criminal justice system friendlier and less menacing.

Morgan's fascination with earthworks and with the relationship between the built environment and nature led to designs involving earth architecture and, later, a book he authored on the subject. In that work Morgan observed: "Frank Lloyd Wright's work respected nature without reservation, but seemingly at a distance; and Le Corbusier elevated his structures on stilts so they safely maintained their departure from nature."[1] William Morgan achieved a middle ground, where modernism coexisted with nature and the environment.

Morgan's application of shaped earth to architecture and landscapes began with the Cowboy Hall of Fame at Harvard's GSD. As his career ascended to its peak, his work increasingly displayed an awareness and sensitivity to the physical shape of the site and responded by including aspects of earth architecture, such as mounding, excavating, and terracing. The architect's use of earth architecture not only created dramatic effects but also helped to develop what Morgan described as "an ecologically sustainable relationship between human beings and their environments, a more enduring relationship rooted in place and in meaning through time."[2]

Morgan was not the only contemporary architect to use earth architecture; his book *Earth Architecture: From Ancient to Modern* provides examples of others, including Frank Lloyd Wright's Second Jacobs House in Middleton, Wisconsin, and Maya Lin's Vietnam Veterans Memorial in Washington, D.C. But Morgan's extensive use of earth architecture uniquely combined with principles of early American and Mesoamerican builders to produce works with a more profound connection to place and to history.

Morgan distinguished himself as a leading, internationally recognized architect, but he simultaneously pursued scholarly research in the field of archaeology. Other architects, of course, have written books about architecture, but we may need to look for genius on the caliber of a Buckminster Fuller to find another architect so prolific in other research pursuits.

Morgan lived by the credo: "The purpose of life is to spend it for something that outlives you," his paraphrase of a William James quotation.

Most of his designs survive, and many continue to be widely admired and respected. These places and buildings indeed outlive him, as do his research and ideas about archaeology and earth architecture. William Morgan found the sweet spot where modernism intersected with nature, with earth, and with humanity's earliest built responses to it.

Figure 134. Morgan worked hard throughout his life, as highlighted in this 2015 photo from the Morgan family.

Afterword

William Morgan's death in 2016 is a natural opportunity for reflection on this man's contributions to architecture. Two architects who are academics and authors of the 1987 and 2002 architectural monographs on Morgan were asked to provide their impressions on William Morgan's impact. Their responses follow.

Remarks by Robert McCarter

Robert McCarter is a practicing architect and the Ruth and Norman Moore Professor of Architecture in the Sam Fox School of Art and Design at Washington University in St. Louis. Before his current appointment he taught at Columbia University from 1986 to 1991, and at the University of Florida, where he was a professor of architecture from 1991 to 2007 and director of the School of Architecture from 1991 to 2001. He is the author of many books, notably *William Morgan: Selected and Current Works* (Images, 2002); *Louis I. Kahn* (Phaidon, 2005); *Frank Lloyd Wright* (Reaktion, 2006); *Understanding Architecture: A Primer on Architecture as Experience* (with Juhani Pallasmaa, Phaidon, 2012); *Carlo Scarpa* (Phaidon, 2013); *Alto* (Phaidon, 2014); *Aldo van Eyck* (Yale University Press, 2015); *Herman Hertzberger* (nai010, 2015); *Steven Holl* (Phaidon, 2015); *The Space Within: Interior Experience as the Origin of Architecture* (Reaktion, 2016); and *Breuer* (Phaidon, 2016).

McCarter provided responses to five questions about Morgan's legacy, contributions, and career.

What do you believe is William Newton Morgan's legacy to American architecture?

William Morgan is one of the very few American architects practicing in the second half of the twentieth century who may be said to have engaged, extended, and reinterpreted the legacy of the two great American modern architects, Frank Lloyd Wright and Louis I. Kahn. Parallel to Wright, Morgan made the engagement of the earth and the horizon, and the construction of refuge and prospect for those who dwell in "the space within," as Wright called it, the primary ordering principle of his domestic works. Parallel to Kahn, Morgan evolved an articulate tectonic language in both cast-in-place and precast concrete that engaged mass and shadow and the alternating rhythm of servant-served spaces in the construction of public spaces that evoked both the timelessly eternal and the timely circumstantial. Paralleling both Wright and Kahn, whom we might call his mentors at a distance, and despite the fact that he was trained by the generation that banished history from the education of architects in America, Morgan nevertheless became an architect possessed of an unparalleled sensitivity to the fundamental place of history in the acts of contemporary design.

In your opinion, what was Morgan's most significant project?

I do not wish to select from among Morgan's house designs, for in fact it is his remarkably consistent evolution across his career of no less than three fully developed domestic building types—structures related to earth, tree, and tower—that sets him apart from almost all his peers. If I had to select a single project, it would be Morgan's Federal Building and Courthouse of 1976–79, which is a public urban building par excellence that exhibits the lessons Morgan learned from his study of historical cities around the world. Morgan believed that architecture has an ethical obligation to the city in which it is built, what he calls the "urban function" of a building. He opposed the contemporary obsession with the optimized "economic development" of our cities, and the deleterious effects this has had on the quality of life for their inhabitants, by endeavoring both to maintain the existing urban fabric and to achieve an appropriate scale, density, and texture in new construction. Morgan established four principles of urban design, exemplified in his Fort Lauderdale courthouse: defining urban street edges, so as to reinforce the public spaces of the city; accommodating parking under or within the building, so as to avoid the destruction of existing fabric to create on-grade parking lots; giving public spaces back to the city, such as roof terraces or shaded courtyards; and developing buildings with low massing (five floors and less), to allow views from taller neighboring structures and to establish the pedestrian street scale found in the greatest cities.

How did William Morgan contribute to Florida architecture, in particular?

Morgan's greatest contribution to Florida architecture was without a doubt his unwavering commitment over his more than fifty-year career to making modern architecture, despite whatever historical pastiche was currently in vogue, as well as his sustained evolution of widely varied and invariably innovative types of architecture, which, despite their variety, were nevertheless always appropriate to their time and place. Morgan was a perfectionist, and was never satisfied that he had found the final answer, and his search continued throughout his career for what he calls the "poetic essence of Florida as a place." This poetic essence has rarely been celebrated in the ever-increasing importation of superficial stylistic "answers" to what, as Morgan has indicated, is a fundamentally experiential question—how should we live in the unique place that is Florida?

What differentiated Morgan from his contemporaries?

Morgan was an architect who evolved from a unique educational and archaeological beginning—studying with Gropius at Harvard and discovering the archaic architecture of Micronesia while serving in the military. He is a rather astonishing triple hybrid: a fundamental modernist whose work has for more than fifty years remained absolutely true to the principles of modern architecture, an accomplished and published historian and archaeologist of ancient architecture heretofore little known or forgotten, and a modern architect who engaged the oldest legacy of place-making in the most contemporary designs. During his career Morgan may be said to have answered the question he asked himself when he started in the 1960s: "What was worth doing now that Wright, Corbu, and Mies were gone?" While this challenge of how to honor and evolve appropriately the legacy of the great early modern architects was not unique to Morgan, his path out of this impasse—his search for what he called "verifiable beginnings in the creative process"—set him apart from his peers.

How is William Newton Morgan's work relevant to contemporary architecture?

In one of its defining attributes, contemporary society has tended to ignore what is near in space and what is distant in time—our local place and our ancient beginnings, while being obsessed by what is distant in space and what is near in time—the universal civilization which has spread around the world and its media-created corollary, the fashionable architectural form. Yet if there is any modern architecture deserving to be called timeless, as Morgan's surely is, it has only come by attending to what is near in space and distant in time; by transforming the modern sense of space through its being built in a particular place, with its history of building engaged in the local climate, landform, vegetation, materials, and methods of construction. In other words, the greatest and most lasting works of modern architecture, such as those of Morgan, are characterized, paradoxically, by being modern while returning to sources. A modernist, trained by the great modern masters, Morgan was nevertheless inspired by the most archaic works of architecture, and it is in this way that he was able, as Paul Ricoeur put it, "to become modern and to return to sources." In his pursuit of modern architecture grounded in the analyses of ancient precedents, Morgan was more like the first generation of modernists, such as Wright, Le Corbusier, and Kahn, who were deeply indebted to the great monuments of history, than he was like his contemporaries, and in this way Morgan avoided many of the failures of his generation in their attempts to reconcile modern design and historical context through formal rather than experiential principles. From both his lifelong studies of archaic architecture and his fifty years of practice engaging contemporary culture and technology, Morgan understood that our experience of place is the fundamental source of meaning in architecture. Morgan's work continues to be relevant to contemporary architecture for the simple but critically important reason that, for him, architecture had integrity when it was inextricably anchored to its place and time, while simultaneously being ordered by principles both universal and timeless, and it is these attributes that allow us to characterize his architecture as being at once ancient and modern.

Remarks by Paul Spreiregen

Paul Spreiregen is an architect and planner as well as an author, teacher, and artist. He is a native of Boston, an honors graduate of the MIT School of Architecture, and was a Fulbright scholar in Italy. He has worked in Milan, Italy; Stockholm, Sweden; and Boston, San Francisco, and New York. He has been based in Washington, D.C., since 1960 and has been involved in architectural and planning projects throughout the United States.

Before beginning his own practice in 1970 he was director of urban design programs at the American Institute of Architects, followed by his position as the first director of architecture and design programs at the then newly established National Endowment for the Arts. He has written, co-authored, or edited a dozen books and numerous articles on architecture and city planning, including the first monograph on Morgan's work, *The Architecture of William Morgan*, which was published in 1987 by the University of Texas Press.

Spreiregen was posed the same questions as Robert McCarter. Following is his response.

Architecture as a Search for Form: William Morgan's Quest

The forms of buildings are, in broad perspective as well as a bit of forgivable license, the product of six determinants. First is the purpose of the building, what it's for. Second is the materials and technology available to make it. Third is a building's site, what it permits or compels. Fourth is climate, again what is permitted or denied. Fifth is the role of embellishment, sometimes symbolic, that gives it meaning in time or culture. And sixth is inventiveness, that of the designers who compose and the builders who construct buildings.

The earliest and most primitive buildings are the product of the first two determinants, purpose and materials, along with a good measure of the site and the climate in which they're built. Taking a broad view of the entire history of building, ever since people began making habitats, and even through to today, those four have been the prime determinants governing building form.

The examples are near infinite. In temperate climates one can still build perfectly useful structures with sticks and thatch, just as have been built since building began. In hot, dry climates mud bricks or natural stone, together with wood beams and a natural impervious roof material, can suffice—and in the same forms of centuries long past. In severely cold climates packed snow alone is enough to build an igloo, the same today as when the technique first came into existence.

The climate in which a building is built and the ground upon which it sits may make little demand on form or may be a major determinant. Sun orientation, precipitation, wind, storms, heat, or cold may pose few demands, or they may pose many. The decision to build on flat or steep terrain or in an earthquake area may or may not be a matter of choice—one permitting a wide range of possibilities, the other severe limitations as well as ingenuity.

Economy in the use of materials and means of construction is an overriding characteristic of all building, particularly so for most of the buildings of history. To take an example, among the earliest dwellings circular forms enclosed the maximum space with the least building material and were especially suited to the needs of nomadic people—teepees or yurts. They are easily erected and just as easily disassembled for travel. In forested areas where lengths of wood are abundant, rectilinear structures are a commonplace and logical outcome. Their simple construction enabled nearly anyone to be a builder. But round or rectilinear, it would not be an exaggeration to suppose that the overwhelming majority of all the buildings of humanity can be seen in this perspective: that they are a product of purpose, materials, site, and climate.

That simple view is not, however, the way more sophisticated and worldly people regard architecture, for as we developed into societies, developed systems of belief, these necessarily found expression in buildings, especially communal buildings. Two predominant early types of buildings required this: temples and palaces. One asserted divine authority, the other temporal. They were only the beginning of a range of types of buildings that required architectural expression to give them meaning, to make a building's purpose manifest. A dome came to signal congress, unity, and so became a symbol of religious concordance as well as government; a spire—aspiration and assertion, hence religious devotion; a shed roof—expedient shelter; a peaked roof—domesticity; a wall—separation and control.

These forms evolved into systems of both symbolic and expressive embellishment that spanned generations, centuries, even millennia. They became the many styles that give identity to a people, a society, a religion, or a culture. Thinking of architecture as this or that style makes it easier to talk about it, especially for today's society, faced as we are with so many things to categorize, to place in convenient order. In heterogeneous modern society it enables people to identify with some long established and long recognized system of values. Those past styles, long in evolution, were ever refined and perfected, confirming their power. American architectural history can usefully be seen as a continuous and ever restless search for values through symbols. Styles have identified our national soul or, more accurately, souls. And the architecture of the past, living on into the present, is a powerful and comforting presence, especially in the face of change that is a constant of life today. But the styles of the past are by no means the sole forms of expression that contemporary society utilizes. Change and inconstancy itself have found expression in architecture—and not just recently but for as long as change and inconstancy have been in play. That, too, has been the basis of an architectural style, indeed many of them, the stuff of much—if not most—of the current critical commentary on architecture.

With such views in mind we can turn to the sixth determinant of architectural form, the inventiveness and ingenuity of the creative mind, the foundation of much of the architecture that characterizes that art in our own time, though not exclusive to it. Looking at architecture through history, viewing all of it that we can know, the inventiveness and ingenuity of the minds that produced all of it reveals a common urge. That is to conceive a form of overall geometric perfection in the whole, a system of order that accommodates all the functions to be served, at the same time binding the entire work into a clear and unified whole. William Morgan's work takes its place in that realm.

To the extent that we can know the creative workings of the mind of a great designer, those of William Morgan are seen through his extensive and most impressive body of works and, tellingly, the studies he did on the architecture of certain cultures of ancient times. His architectural work is well documented in two books, *The Architecture of William Morgan* by Paul D. Spreiregen (1987) and *William Morgan: Selected and Current Works* by Robert McCarter (2002). His studies were published in five books, *Prehistoric Architecture in the Eastern United States* (1980), *Prehistoric Architecture in Micronesia* (1988), *Ancient Architecture of the Southwest* (1994), *Precolumbian Architecture in Eastern North America* (1999), and *Earth Architecture* (2008).

What emerges from a joint examination of Morgan's architectural works and his scholarly studies of ancient architecture is his unwavering impulse to perfection of form. As clear is his dedication to engaging the form of the earth upon which his buildings rested and sometimes burrowed. In short, perfection of form wedded with the integration of site and building was his organizing mantra. Not all his buildings offered the opportunity to address both. Neither could the effort have been without struggle and, on occasion, compromise.

William Morgan held to this course during a tumultuous time in architectural design, a period that explored such movements as postmodernism, which toyed arbitrarily with the forms of past and present, or deconstructivism, which celebrated irrationality and confusion. Morgan would have none of it. Such movements are a betrayal of what he believed architecture stood for. One can argue that those movements liberated architecture from stultification, that they enabled a fresh direction, such as found in the recent work of the Norwegian architectural firm Snøhetta, the Swiss firm Herzog and de Meuron, or the Danish firm BIG, and a good many others. But the work of these groups is never arbitrary or capricious, certainly not irrational.

Morgan's approach, as seen in his designs, had two directions. One was to let a building be what it wanted to be, paraphrasing Louis Kahn. The other, as mentioned, was his predilection to perfection of form, to geometric purity.

The first is to let a building's layout and form emanate from its program, relating its various spaces one to another, the whole to its site, all the while being mindful of site form and climate, and doing all this without trying to fit all the parts into some pristine geometry. That is the dictum of letting form follow function. The example of his work that illustrates this most cogently is his unbuilt 1982–84 design for the Creek House in Austin, Texas, a 16,000-square-foot residence. It also recalls Frank Lloyd Wright's principle of a building being "of the site, not on it." The layout of the Creek House flowed readily from its program and site, but as a design configuration it stands almost alone in Morgan's work.

Instead Morgan pursued the more challenging second direction—pristine, organizing, and all-encompassing geometrical form. In these efforts he most often employed symmetry on a central axis, as in his own residence (1971–72) and the Dunehouses (1974–75), both in Atlantic Beach, Florida; sometimes bilateral symmetry, as in Hilltop House (1972–75) in Brooksville, Florida, and the Medical Clinic (1981–82) in Jacksonville, Florida; and on occasion pinwheel symmetry, as in the Pinwheel Apartments (1966–67) in Jacksonville, Florida, and Ten Central Park (1982–83) in Stuart, Florida. This all but turns the dictum of letting form follow function on its head, choosing instead to have function yield to form. In master hands such as Morgan's this can succeed handsomely. But the success of this approach depends greatly on the building's program, its spatial and functional requirements. It works best in more modest smaller buildings, or where the building program is fairly simple, as in his own house and the Dunehouses, or for larger buildings with many repetitive components, such as the Westinghouse Headquarters (1980–83) in Orlando, Florida. When the requirements are more numerous, and hence more complex, compromises become inevitable. And while they are generally acceptable they do have their cost. Sometimes an entry or a stair is not counterbalanced by a like form. Sometimes symmetry requires a certain space to be a bit too large or too small in order to match its counterpart, or not oriented to sunlight in the most advantageous way. In the world of architectural design this is a tricky path to tread.

A story about Frank Lloyd Wright illustrates the challenge—one might say quandary—of trying to fit programmatic requirements into an overruling geometric system. From time to time Wright liked to lay out a building design on a grid, or module, usually a system of squares of a certain size. Sometimes he tried triangular modules. In one such instance, his apprentices watching as he worked, Wright broke the grid and simply drew in what was needed, completely ignoring the grid. When one of the apprentices questioned this, the master's response was, "I make the rules. I break them."

All this is to illustrate the degree of challenge that William Morgan so willingly took on, and in which he so brilliantly succeeded, leaving a heritage of work that stands with pride and distinction in the flow of American architecture. His memory will live through the gifts of his work.

But let me end on a personal note, with a rejoinder to my observations so far. Architecture is meant to be experienced, to be approached, entered, seen sequentially, walked through, worked in, viewed, touched—in sum, to be lived in. Words and pictures are not architecture. At best they may be gateways to its understanding and appreciation. I had the pleasure of staying at the Morgans' house in Atlantic Beach with Bill and his wife, Bunny, when I was writing the book on his work back in the 1980s. That told me a good deal of what I needed to know about what he was about. I hope readers, similarly, may visit and experience some of his many public buildings to get their flavor. For all, readers of his books and visitors to his buildings, I hope my comments have amplified a much-deserved appreciation of his splendid achievements.

Acknowledgments

This book reflects the contributions of many wonderful people.

William Morgan contributed most of the information contained within these pages. His wife, Bunny Morgan, tirelessly supported her husband's career from his time at the Harvard Graduate School of Design up until his last days in early 2016. An organizational dynamo, she devoted her energy and optimism to this project and kept it moving through the ups and downs of her late husband's medical condition and numerous other challenges and distractions. Bunny was William Morgan's biggest promoter from the architect's years in graduate school up to and beyond his death. Her support, encouragement, and photographic memory contributed vastly to this project's completion.

Brad Chesivoir, whom I consider my oldest and dearest friend, is a talented photographer who has had a long professional career in Washington. Many of the contemporary photos in this work reflect the outcome of his several successful visits to Florida as well as his intuitive vision for capturing and conveying the unique beauty and striking character of a place. Photographers Charles Badland and Antony Rieck contributed photographs of the U.S. Courthouse in Tallahassee and the Quelch-Gendzier Residence, respectively..

Three marvelous people were kind enough to read and edit drafts of this book. Chris Silver, of the University of Florida's College of Design, Construction and Planning, read an early draft and provided useful comments. Adam Weissmann, a congressional speechwriter, provided edits and useful suggestions that contributed mightily toward enhancing clarity. Florida journalist Susan Cooper Eastman has long been a supporter of my efforts to increase awareness of modern architecture. Susan's edits have made this book much more readable.

William Morgan's brother, Dr. Thomas E. Morgan Jr., provided detail to flesh out some of the particulars of his brother's early years. Morgan's Harvard classmates Moe Finegold and Jeremiah O'Leary also helped with details about the school and about Morgan's later projects. Morgan's son Dylan contributed helpful insights into his father's life and career.

The Architectural Archive of the University of Florida's George A. Smathers Libraries preserves the drawings, photographs, papers, and models of many of the state's most important architects, including William Morgan. John Nemmers and the archive's staff helpfully provided access to this vast resource as well as additional assistance in support of this project. Anzhelika Arbatskaya worked with Nemmers to provide important images that are reproduced in this book. Cynthia Peterson, formerly associated with the archive, deserves enormous credit for organizing and cataloguing this material to make it accessible and useful to researchers like me. As director of the university's School of Architecture, Martha Kohen cofounded the archive in 2004 and was able—after five attempts—to convince William Morgan to donate his architectural renderings, technical drawings, models, and papers.

Ines Zalduendo at the Frances Loeb Library at Harvard's Graduate School of Design provided access to Morgan's student projects and other archival resources.

Four former architects at Morgan's firm shared their insights: Tom Duke, Bill Ebert, David Engdahl, and Tom McCrary.

The inhabitants of several houses designed by Morgan were helpful and welcoming. These include Ron and Marchant Martin; Maxwell and Edna Dickinson; Doctors Virginia Quelch and Mark Gendzier; George and Kitty Goodloe; Francis and Diane Lott; Rebekah Beller and Richard Wolfe; and David Robortaccio. Additionally, Janice and Bill McClure provided a tour of the beautiful and important Rawls Residence. Gary Dickinson of the Jacksonville Sheriff's

Office provided a morning-long tour of the Police Memorial Building and provided access to restricted areas, where Brad Chesivoir captured some great photographs. Petty Officer Mark Treen and Public Affairs Officer Scott Bassett of the Kings Bay Submarine Base in Georgia welcomed us with an extensive tour of William Morgan's spectacular twin pyramids, the facility's centerpiece. Lee Meadows and the staff at Meadows, Incorporated, provided access to the E.L.K. Oil Company Building as well as information about that early Morgan office building. The University of Miami's Jean-François Lejeune shared important material on the Federal Building and Courthouse in Fort Lauderdale.

My wife, Stephanie, and my daughters, Eva and Sophie, provided love and support, for which I am always thankful.

I am profoundly grateful to Martha Kohen, Robert McCarter, and Paul Spreiregen for their thoughtful contributions to this book.

I first became friends with William Morgan in 2006 as I organized a tour of modernist architectural sites in Jacksonville, Florida. During occasional visits I enjoyed discussing architecture and ideas with him. His original mind and prodigious gift for telling a good story made for joyful visits, but the experiences also made me think it would be useful to share some of that with people who didn't know Morgan—and perhaps even some who did.

I bring to the book a lifelong interest in urbanism, planning, and architecture that led me to pursue both master's and doctoral degrees in city planning, from Harvard and the University of Florida, respectively. As president of the Florida chapter of Docomomo, an international organization for the documentation and conservation of buildings, sites, and neighborhoods of the modern movement, I came to know many important contributors to the built environment of postwar Florida, including William Morgan, who clearly was one its stars.

Notes

Foreword

1. Paul Spreiregen, *The Architecture of William Morgan* (Austin: University of Texas Press, 1987).
2. Robert McCarter, *William Morgan: Selected and Current Works,* Master Architect Series no. 6 (Victoria, Australia: Images Publishing Group, 2002).
3. William Morgan, *Prehistoric Architecture in the Eastern United States* (Cambridge, Mass.: MIT Press, 1980); William Morgan, *Prehistoric Architecture in Micronesia* (Austin: University of Texas Press, 1988); William Morgan, *Ancient Architecture of the Southwest* (Austin: University of Texas Press, 1994); William Morgan, *Precolumbian Architecture in Eastern North America* (Gainesville: University Press of Florida, 1999).
4. William Morgan, *Earth Architecture from Ancient to Modern* (Gainesville: University Press of Florida, 2008).
5. Jane Jacobs, *The Nature of Economies* (New York: Vintage Books, 2000).

Introduction

1. See, for example, Le Corbusier, "A house is a machine for living in," in *Towards a New Architecture*, 95.
2. Le Corbusier's given name was Charles Édouard Jeanneret.
3. Blake, *Master Builders*, xiv.
4. Spreiregen's *Architecture of William Morgan* presents Morgan's work chronologically. McCarter, in *William Morgan: Selected and Current Works*, grouped the projects into three categories: Earth Projects, Tree Projects, and Tower Projects.
5. After the French term *béton brut*, translated as "raw concrete."

Chapter 1. Early Years

1. Morgan, *Ancient Architecture of the Southwest,* vii.

Chapter 2. Harvard College

1. Cronin's bar and restaurant was a fixture on Mt. Auburn Street in Cambridge between 1942 and 1978.

Chapter 3. Navy Service

1. Giedion, *Space, Time and Architecture,* 405.
2. Blake, *Master Builders*, 352.
3. The original hotel came down in 1968.
4. Morgan and Morgan, *Prehistoric Architecture in Micronesia*, 119.
5. Ibid., 133–35.
6. Hines and Neutra, *Richard Neutra and the Search for Modern Architecture,* 231.
7. The school is listed on the National Register of Historic Places. The Register's Statement of Significance notes: "The F. Q. Sanchez Elementary School is of 'exceptional importance' as a historical modern structure built during the International Modern movement. The architect Richard Neutra designed the school to be an important function of the village. The school is not only functional, but accessible (the kids walk to school) and consciously interactive with the environment. The residents believe that the school brings the community together."

Chapter 4. Harvard Graduate School of Design

1. Peter, *Masters of Modern Architecture*, 27.
2. The building was completed in 1958.
3. Rohan, *Architecture of Paul Rudolph*, 40.
4. Saxon, "Serge Chermayeff, 95, Architect; Taught at Harvard and Yale."
5. Rohan, *Architecture of Paul Rudolph*, 183.
6. The AIA is the American Institute of Architects.
7. 27 Church Street, across the street from Rudolph's office.
8. Pearlman, "Joseph Hudnut's Other Modernism at the 'Harvard Bauhaus,'" 473.
9. Ibid., 452.
10. Ibid., 473–74.
11. Ibid., 471.
12. Morgan, *Earth Architecture: From Ancient to Modern*, 1.
13. Morgan, *Prehistoric Architecture in the Eastern United States*, viii.
14. Kapelos, *Competing Modernisms*, 55.

Chapter 5. A Career Begins

1. Drew, "A Conundrum in Time: Medieval and Modern Pavilions," 60.
2. Domin and King, *Paul Rudolph: The Florida Houses*, 38.
3. Harvard University, Graduate School of Design, "Wheelwright Prize."
4. Ibid.
5. "Starting a Successful Practice," 136.
6. Ennis, "Imagination (and Cash) Win Citations for Best Home Design," 215.
7. Hochstim, *Florida Modern*.
8. Ibid., 260.
9. Rohan, *Architecture of Paul Rudolph*, 151–64.
10. "Interpod, by William Morgan Architect," 27.
11. "Two Residential Developments in Florida," 156–58.

Chapter 6. The Practice Expands

1. Since 1998 it has been known as the Florida Museum of Natural History. In 1998 its exhibit space was relocated to a new building, Powell Hall.
2. University of Florida Oral History Program, April 5, 1984.
3. Von Eckardt, "Designing In, Under, Around and With Earth."
4. Owen, "Playboy Pad on the Beach," 131–33.
5. Jim DeStefano, "Great Achievements," 72–75.

Chapter 7. Trailblazing in Earth Architecture

1. E.L.K. Oil Company Building, in Jacksonville, Florida.
2. Dean, "Underground Architecture."

Chapter 8. Bold Design on a Large Scale

1. Crooks, *Jacksonville: The Consolidation Story*, 71–76.
2. Hoyt, "Breaking Down the Battlements," 122.
3. Lejeune, "William Morgan in Florida."
4. "Celebration of Justice: The Federal Building, Courthouse in Ft. Lauderdale, Florida."
5. Gibson, "Push for New Federal Courthouse in Ft. Lauderdale Moves Forward."
6. Gibson, "Broward Leaders Lobby for Port, Courthouse and Streetcar Funds."
7. Now known as the Hyatt Regency Jacksonville Riverfront.

Chapter 9. Author and Architect

1. Morgan, *Prehistoric Architecture in the Eastern United States*, viii.
2. Heyden and Gendrop, *Pre-Columbian Architecture of Mesoamerica*.

Chapter 10. More Recent Projects

1. A more recent Morgan-designed project was built nearby on Amelia Island. However, its owners insist on privacy and anonymity, which are respected here.
2. Morgan, *Earth Architecture: From Ancient to Modern*, 6.

Chapter 11. Final Thoughts

1. Morgan, *Earth Architecture: From Ancient to Modern*, 6.
2. Ibid., 6.

Bibliography

Blake, Peter. *The Master Builders*. New York: Norton, 1976.

"Celebration of Justice: The Federal Building, Courthouse in Fort Lauderdale, Florida." *Architectural Record* 166 (1979): 81–86.

Corbusier, Le. *Towards a New Architecture*. New York: Dover Publications, 1986.

Crooks, James B. *Jacksonville: The Consolidation Story, from Civil Rights to the Jaguars*. Gainesville: University Press of Florida, 2004.

Dean, Andrea. "Underground Architecture." *AIA Journal* 67 (1978): 38–41.

DeStefano, Jim. "Great Achievements: Horst Berger." *Structure* 14, no. 11 (2007): 72–75. http://www.structuremag.org/wp-content/uploads/2014/08/D-GrAchievements-Berger-Nov071.pdf.

Domin, Christopher, and Joseph King. *Paul Rudolph: The Florida Houses*. New York: Princeton Architectural Press, 2005.

Drew, Philip. "A Conundrum in Time: Medieval and Modern Pavilions." *Architectural Theory Review* 11, no. 2 (2006): 53–65.

Ennis, Thomas. "Imagination (and Cash) Win Citations for Best Home Design." *New York Times*, June 6, 1965.

Gibson, William. "Broward Leaders Lobby for Port, Courthouse and Streetcar Funds." *Sun-Sentinel*, September 30, 2015.

———. "Push for New Federal Courthouse in Ft. Lauderdale Moves Forward." *Sun-Sentinel*, May 21, 2015.

Giedion, S. 1967. *Space, Time and Architecture: The Growth of a New Tradition*. 5th ed., rev. and enl. Cambridge: Harvard University Press, 1967.

Harvard University, Graduate School of Design. "Wheelwright Prize." http://www.gsd.harvard.edu/architecture/fellowships-prizes-and-travel-programs/wheelwright-prize/.

Heyden, D., and P. Gendrop. *Pre-Columbian Architecture of Mesoamerica*. New York: H. N. Abrams, 1975.

Hines, Thomas S., and Richard Joseph Neutra. *Richard Neutra and the Search for Modern Architecture: A Biography and History*. Berkeley: University of California Press, 1994.

Hochstim, J. *Florida Modern: Residential Architecture 1945–1970*. New York: Rizzoli, 2004.

Hoyt, Charles King. "Breaking Down the Battlements: Jacksonville's New Police Headquarters." *Progressive Architecture* 59 (1978): 122.

"Interpod, by William Morgan Architect." *Arts & Architecture* 84, no. 4 (1967): 27.

Jacobs, Jane. *The Nature of Economies*. New York: Vintage Books, 2000.

Kapelos, George. *Competing Modernisms: Toronto's New City Hall and Square*. Halifax, Nova Scotia: Dalhousie Architectural Press, 2015.

Lejeune, Jean-François. "William Morgan in Florida: Tropical Brutalism in the Age of Consensus." Presentation at the 14th International Conference of Docomomo, Lisbon, September 6–9, 2016.

McCarter, Robert. *William Morgan: Selected and Current Works*. Master Architect Series no. 6. Victoria, Australia: Images Publishing Group, 2002.

Morgan, William N. *Ancient Architecture of the Southwest*. Austin: University of Texas Press, 1994.

———. *Earth Architecture: From Ancient to Modern*. Gainesville: University Press of Florida, 2008.

———. Interview by Sid Johnston, University of Florida Oral History Program, April 5, 1984.

———. *Precolumbian Architecture in Eastern North America*. Gainesville: University Press of Florida, 1999.
———. *Prehistoric Architecture in the Eastern United States*. Cambridge, Mass.: MIT Press, 1980.
Morgan, W. N. *Prehistoric Architecture in Micronesia*. Austin: University of Texas Press, 1988.
Owen, Tom. "Playboy Pad on the Beach." *Playboy*, August 1975, 133–35.
———. "Return of the Caveman." *Playboy*, February 1977, 193.
Pearlman, Jill. "Joseph Hudnut's Other Modernism at the 'Harvard Bauhaus.'" *Journal of the Society of Architectural Historians* 56, no. 4 (1997): 452–77.
Peter, John. *Masters of Modern Architecture*. New York: G. Braziller, 1958.
Rohan, T. M. *The Architecture of Paul Rudolph*. New Haven: Yale University Press, 2014.
Saini, Balwant, and Alison Moore. "Traditional Architecture in the Pacific." http://espace.library.uq.edu.au/view/UQ:13635/bs_tradarchpac.pdf.
Saxon, Wolfgang. "Serge Chermayeff, 95, Architect; Taught at Harvard and Yale." *New York Times*, May 10, 1996.
Spreiregen, Paul D. *The Architecture of William Morgan*. Austin: University of Texas Press, 1987.
"Starting a Successful Practice." *Architectural Record* 46 (1965): 136.
"Two Residential Developments in Florida." *Architectural Record* 48 (1967): 156–58.
von Eckardt, Wolf. "Designing In, Under, Around and With Earth." *Washington Post*, April 8, 1972.
Wagman, Jules L. *On Target: The First Twenty-Five Years of the Haskell Company*. Jacksonville: Haskell Company, 1990.
Wittkower, R. "Brunelleschi and 'Proportion in Perspective.'" *Journal of the Warburg and Courtauld Institutes* 16 (1953): 275–91.

Richard Shieldhouse is a planner, preservationist, and tourism expert. He has a master's degree in city and regional planning from Harvard University and a doctorate in design, construction, and planning from the University of Florida. He lives in Jacksonville, Florida, and works as a transportation consultant.